RATAN TATA
A COMPLETE BIOGRAPHY

The Logos used on Cover are owned by
Tata Sons

RATAN TATA
A COMPLETE BIOGRAPHY

A.K. GANDHI

PRABHAT
PAPERBACKS

Publisher
PRABHAT PAPERBACKS
4/19 Asaf Ali Road, New Delhi–110 002
Ph. 23289555 • 23289666 • 23289777 • Helpline/ 🟢 7827007777
e-mail: prabhatbooks@gmail.com • Website: www.prabhatbooks.com

© Reserved

Edition
First, 2021

Price
Three Hundred Rupees only

ISBN 978-93-5521-174-3

Printed at
AMSONS, Sahibabad

RATAN TATA A COMPLETE BIOGRAPHY
by A.K. Gandhi

ISBN 978-93-5521-174-3

₹ 300.00

Dedicated to the father of

TATA Group

'Bharat Ratna' awardee

Shri J.R.D.TATA

who gave a new definition and direction

to entrepreneurship

Author's Note

The brightest star of the Indian industrial world, the surveyor of a huge industrial empire like the Tata Group, Ratan Tata, also has a distinctive place in the world industry.

In the current environment, his role and leadership have been a commendable contribution in making the Tata Group an important institution not only indigenously but also abroad.

When J.R.D. Tata was given the responsibility of industrial heritage by Ratan Tata, he had a tough challenge to prove his competence and industrial understanding. He had to prove that he became the chairman of the Tata group because of his ability and talent not because of his links with the Tata family. The then influential men of the Tata group, looked at Ratan Tata with suspicion and derision. His critics were also no less active. But Ratan Tata amazed everyone with his unique talent in a few years. Under his leadership, the Tata group marked its strong presence at the international level. Not only this, he was also awarded the title of 'Indian Henry Ford'. He was addressed as the pioneer of India's road to revolution. 'Lakhtakiya Nano' is an outstanding example of his talent, perseverance and foresight.

It is also noteworthy that all of the yugdrashta pioneers of this clan from Jamsetji Tata, the founder of the group to Ratan Tata's predecessor J.R.D. Tata have had a distinctive role in establishing, refining and modifying the industrial heritage which Ratan Tata is looking after today.

The foundations, work environment and norms that these leaders had established also have a strong place in leading the Tata Group to its present stage. Therefore, it would be appropriate to mention here all the shinning stars of the 'Tata family', who worked relentlessly for its operation and progressive growth. Only then a complete and accurate assessment of Ratan Tata's personality and actions is possible. Keeping this fact in mind, necessary material about them is presented in the beginning of the book. Hopefully, the book will prove to be inspiring and beneficial for the readers.

— Author

Contents

Author's Note	7
❖ Family Background	11
❖ Jamsetji Tata	14
❖ Sir Dorabji Tata	22
❖ Lady Meherbai	25
❖ Ratan Dadabhai Tata	27
❖ Sir Ratan Tata	30
❖ Lady Nawazbai	34
❖ Naval Hormusji Tata	36
❖ J.R.D. Tata	42
❖ Ratan Tata	47
❖ Tata Group's Journey Under the Leadership of Ratan Tata	50
❖ Ratan Tata's Foresight	54
❖ Strong Intention	56
❖ Some famous Tata Owned Companies and Brands	61
❖ Tata Steel	62
❖ Tata Chemicals	65
❖ Tata Motors	67
❖ Tata Tea	72
❖ Tata Power	75
❖ Tata Consultancy Services	77
❖ Tata Teleservices	82

- Tata Communications ------- 85
- Tata Sky ------- 86
- Titan Industries ------- 87
- Tanishq ------- 88
- Tata Technologies ------- 90
- Voltas Limited ------- 91
- Tata A.I.G. ------- 92
- The Taj Group ------- 93
- Large Acquisitions of Tata Group Across the Sea ------- 98
- Some Important Achievements ------- 100
- Acquisition of Jaguar Land Rover ------- 103
- Entry of Land Rover Cars in the Indian Market ------- 106
- Chairman of Tata Sons ------- 108
- Tata Group: Some Facts ------- 109
- Honors Received by Ratan Tata ------- 112
- Paramount in Generosity ------- 114
- Contribution of Sir Ratan Tata ------- 116
- Sir Ratan Tata Trust ------- 120
- Sir Dorabji Tata Trust ------- 123
- Relief Work During Disasters ------- 126
- Nano: Manufacturing of People's Car ------- 129
- Singur Land Acquisition Dispute ------- 136
- New Centre for Setting Up Nano Project: Sanand (Gujarat) ------- 139
- Entry of Nano in the Market ------- 141
- Ratan Tata: A Gentle and Dignified Personality ------- 143
- Something More about Ratan Tata ------- 147
- Top Motivational Quotes/Inspiring ------- 150
- Success Principles of Ratan Tata ------- 161

Family Background

The Parsi community is believed to have lived in Persia (present-day Iran) hundreds of years ago. Their people gradually spread to all the countries of the world based on trade and industry. In the same sequence, the Parsi's also arrived in India centuries ago. Despite being spread across many regions of the world, their number is quite less. They are considered particularly the worshipers of fire, but they also worship Sun, Moon, and Air. In the old times, the Parsi community gave special emphasis on archery, horse riding, and character-building. Changes in many areas were inevitable over time. Nevertheless, their perseverance on the purity of community and character is more or less still intact. As a community inclined towards preserving their heritage they do not encourage marriage outside their own societies, even if they married in close relationships, so that the purity of the caste could be preserved. This taboo is still present to a large extent. Even mentally, Parsi's are very strong and their behavior is dignified. Their performance in knowledge and science and their field of work is generally good.

Parsi's have created a special place for themselves in the Indian society. They have earned the respect they truly deserve. Parsi's have played an important role not only in the industrial world but also in contemporary social activities. Along with making a significant contribution to the economic development of the country, they have discharged the national and social commitments with efficiency and integrity. Despite having minority status, they have not redeemed it for political-economic benefit but have focused on creating opportunities for their growth through hard work and dedication. This is an important characteristic quality of them.

Navsari is also one of the oldest towns in Gujarat. Centuries ago, a group of Parsi's came and settled here. For some time, the region was also under the influence of Parsi's, later it was taken over by the Muslim invaders. At the time of independence of the country in 1947, this area was under the princely state of Baroda. Navsari has been the home of a large class of Parsi's. Dadabhai Naoroji, who was elected as a member of the British Parliament during the British rule, was also born in Navsari.

Navsari was also the residence of Nausherwanji Tata, father of Jamsetji Tata, the founder of the

Tata Gharana. Jamsetji Tata's birthplace is Navsari. Today their residence is preserved as a memorial.

Jamsetji's father Nausherwanji belonged to that branch of the Parsi community, which was involved in hieratic work. His ancestors had been doing the same work for many generations. Therefore, they were also counted among the respected classes of the society. With the changing times, the uneasiness of change started in all societies. The Tata family of the Parsi community also could not remain untouched by this. Nausherwanji was the first man in the Tata family who instead of sticking to centuries-old tradition and values, thought of going ahead and doing something new. As a result, he decided to make business his field of work and means of livelihood.

The town Navsari was quite backward at that time, so to fulfill his dream, he found Bombay perfectly suitable and left Navsari and left for Bombay. He started his work with business and banking. Although this was a new and unfamiliar area for him, still he was slowly progressing in this area with steady steps. As the experience grew, his thinking also got a new direction and he took a concrete decision for the future that they have to lead their future generations in this direction only.

His only son Jamset was in Navsari at that time. To give a practical form to his dream, he also called him to Bombay, so that he could be raised properly and with experience in the proper business environment, he could also get business skills, which would prove helpful in shaping his future.

❏❏

Jamsetji Tata

The leading man of the Indian industrial world, Yugdrashta Jamset Nausherwanji Tata, was born on March 3, in Navsari in a family of Parsi Priests. He is called the father of Indian industry. He was the only son of his father. His childhood was spent in Navsari.

When Jamsetji was 13, his father started an export business in Bombay. He made his debut in Bombay at the age of 14. According to Parsi tradition, he was married at the age of 16 to Hirabai (10 years). Nausherwanji wanted to his son to get higher education, so at the age of 17, he was admitted to Elphinstone College. After a few years he completed his college education as a 'Green Scholar' (equivalent to graduation). His attachment to literature and books continued throughout his life. After completing his education, his father enrolled him into his business and started to teach him the technicalities of operation.

In 1859, his father sent him on a business trip to Hong Kong, where he worked to open a branch of his family firm and was busy with other related tasks. He lived there until 1863.

Debut in the Industrial Field

At the age of 29, he started a personal trading firm in 1868 with a capital of rupees 2100. Through this, Jamsetji and his partners got the contract to supply some military equipment abroad. There was a sufficient amount of profit in this which inspired him to start his work in the field of textiles. In partnership with some of his friends, he bought an old oil mill in Bombay in 1869 and converted it into a textile (cloth manufacturing) factory. He took up the task of managing it himself and within few years he changed it into a working factory. Two years later he sold it to a textile businessman at profit. He named it 'Alexandra Cotton Mill'.

In 1872, Jamasetji once again turned towards England. This time his aim was to study the industry there, especially the textile business in Lancashire. He was keen to develop the Indian textile industry.

At that time there was about a dozen textile mills in Bombay and it was considered a suitable place for textile mills. But contrary to this thinking, Jamsetji chose Nagpur, in central India to set up his factory. Thus, they also got the benefit of the railway facilities established up to that area at that time. While choosing Nagpur city, he kept in mind three main facts - cotton production, railway facilities and fuel and water supply situation.

In 1874, he started 'The Central Indian Spinning, Weaving And Manufacturing Company' with a capital of 15,00,000 investing capital along with his friends. After declaring Queen Victoria as Queen of India on 1 January,1877, the 'Empires Mill' was started in Nagpur.

The yarn cloth mill of Nagpur also worked as laboratory for Jamsetji. Here he focused on every single details of its development. Special focus was given on new experiments of technology and labour welfare. Quality of the fabric was also improved by substituting the most advanced American machinery of that time. He made new facilities like the pension fund in the year 1886 and accident compensation in the year 1895 for his workers. In this way he surpassed his competitors.

Encouraged by his primary successes, in 1886 only he thought of purchasing a defamed ailing mill. At the age of 47 he accepted the challenge of turning this sick mill into a healthy one. This mill, named 'Swadeshi Cotton Mill' on the lines of Swadeshi movement, was mainly supported by Indian shareholders. He invested in it willingly. But later on, some situations were such that even after two years the mill could not declare dividend. Due to some reasons and rumours, prices of the share fell. The name of 'Tata' was at stake. When the banks also refused to give loans Jamsetji collected capital by selling some share of his Family Trust and Empires Mill and invested it in the indigenous cotton mill. This had a desired effect and the stock prices went up. He provided the best services of his best minds and skilled employees to the Swadeshi Cotton Mill and within a few years transformed it into a high-grade textile mill. Soon the fabric manufactured in it started to get exported to China, Korea, Japan and Middle East countries.

When Jamsetji realized that bulk of company's profit was spent in paying the freight for water transportation of goods from Bombay to China and Japan branches he took the initiative to change the situation. At that time, this waterway was predominantly monopolized by three companies, which always kept their rates high. So Jamsetji turned to a Japanese steam navigation company called 'Nippon Yusen Kaisha' to facilitate cheap transportation. Monopoly companies opposed this, but Jamsetji fought it out and emerged victorious. In June 1896, these companies were forced to reduce their freight to a reasonable and competitive level.

Jamsetji was fully aware that the industrial revolution is a fundamental requirement for industrial success, so he was determined to use the advanced technology and methods prevalent in the industrial sector. At that time, the work of increasing the network of railways and telegraph to connect different regions of India was going on. The Tata group made meaningful use of it in expanding its industrial empire.

Entry into Iron and Steel Industry

During his stay in England itself Jamsetji had decided that he would definitely establish an Iron and Steel industry in India. In view of the circumstances of that time this thought was itself a brave work. India's then British government was also not interested in developing big businesses in India. Therefore, the policies of the government were automatically a road block. But Jamsetji was unstoppable to embody his imagination.

In 1901, Jamsetji focused on the Indian steel industry which was at its primary stage at that time and produced a small amount of steel. In this work he took help of British and American surveyors. The main name among them is that of an American Charles Page Perin, who spent many years in India for the Geological Survey of India to find iron deposits. Later on, a few Indian surveyors also supported him. He travelled to European countries and America for technical advice and information of steel making. He wanted to undertake iron refining on a large scale so he invested a large amount of money on this project. Before this plan of Jamsetji could take shape, he died in Germany in 1904. He had two sons to decorate, cherish, develop and fulfil his incomplete dreams, elder son Dorabji and the younger son Ratan and to support both of them Jamsetji's cousin R.D. Tata was present. Before he died, he had expressed his wish to his cousin R.D. Tata, son Dorab and other close relatives to carry forward the work he had started. If they could not do so then at least should preserve to continue the work done so far.

Jamsetji's dream of steel making came true when the Tata Steel and Iron Company was established in 1907 at Sakchi, 150 miles west of Calcutta. This place was suitable for raw materials, coal, water supply and transportation, so the company grew rapidly. On 16 February 1912, the first steel ingot was produced from the Sakchi plant in a happy atmosphere. Today it is a major steel industry in the country. The imagination Jamsetji had for his steel city was given full respect in the making of Jamshedpur (Sakchi).

Construction of Taj Mahal Hotel

Jamsetji built India's best hotel the Taj Mahal Hotel in Bombay. A huge amount of money was spent in its construction. His purpose behind its construction was to promote tourism by attracting travellers to India. He himself bought the furnishings of the hotel during his travels. The hotel was well equipped with all the facilities in line with European standards of that time. In this, all necessary arrangements were made, including a soda and ice factory, washing and polishing machines, laundry, elevators and electric generators. It was inaugurated in 1903. At that time, it was the first building in Bombay which was lighted. It had American fans and Turkey styled bathrooms. English butlers were appointed for the kitchen. Overall, the hotel had all the facilities that were present in the world's best-known hotels.

Jamsetji's Public Welfare Works

Jamshetji was deeply connected with the rites of

benevolence. For this, in 1892, he established the J.N. Tata Trust. He established a fund for higher education. Under this, he started sending deserving students abroad for higher education. Under this scheme, many of India's early engineers, surgeons, physician, barristers and ICS officers were benefited.

In 1898, he presented his fourteen buildings and a large sum of money and four properties for the establishment of the Post Graduate Institute for Scientific Research. Although his dream could not be fulfilled during his life time due to the high-handedness of the British Government, but his sons fulfilled it after his death. Thus in 1911, the institute was established in Bangalore, which was a joint collaboration of Tata, Government of India and Government of Mysore. Initially it had only three major departments — General and Applied Chemistry, Electro Technology Chemistry and Organic Chemistry. Later, many other departments were added to it from time to time.

Like Tata Steel, Jamshedpur, the Indian Institute, Bangalore served as a centre from which later many other branches—Central Food and Technological Research Institute, Mysore; Lac Research Institute, Ranchi; National Aeronautical Laboratory, Bangalore bloomed. It also contributed to the establishment and development of many other institutions.

Endowed with Vision and Intuition

Jamsetji will also be remembered for his vision, intuition and for imbibing and implementing new ideas and fantasies. He used it not only to develop his business but also to improve the lives of the countrymen. He gave importance to innovation. He was the first person to use rubber tires in the wagon. He was the first automobile driver in Bombay. He donated generously for essential works. He was steeped in high social ideals. He made new arrangements for labour facilities and their welfare in the field of labour and introduced new rules, which would not have been in the imagination of anyone else. Those reforms were implemented abroad after many decades. Many reforms came into existence only after many movements. The whole country still respects him and remembers him with gratitude.

On January 7, 1965, the Indian Postal and Telegraph Department commenced a postage stamp in honour of Jamsetji. It shows the gratitude of the country for his services in industrialization of the country.

◻◻

Sir Dorabji Tata

Dorabji was the elder son of Jamsetji Tata, who, after his death, took care of his legacy and took it to new heights. His younger brother Sir Ratan Tata and Jamsetji's cousin Ratan Dadabhai Tata gave full support in this task. It was his optimism and strong will power that helped the Tata Group overcome every difficulty and he managed to take the company to new heights by giving form to his father's dreams.

Dorabji was born in 1859 and got his primary education at the Proprietary High School in Bombay. He was then sent to England. At the age of 18, he attended Gonville and Caius College in Cambridge.

He also performed well in sports while studying at Cambridge and won several awards in cricket and football. Dorabji returned to India in 1879 and enrolled at St. Xavier's College, Bombay. After completion of his education, he started his work as a journalist at the 'Bombay Gazette'. Gradually he became interested in his father's business and in 1884 he entered the ancestral business. He was accommodated in the cotton division.

Jamsetji wanted his son Dorab to meet the high scholar and respected Dr. H.J. Bhabha, who lived with his daughter Meherbai. When he reached there, he also met Bhabha's daughter Meher. This meeting later ended into their marriage. At the time of this marriage in 1897, Dorabji was 38 years old, while Meherbai was only 18 years old.

Dorabji had all the qualities of the Tata family for which they were well-known. These qualities are - leading, leadership and achievement of purpose. It was the result of his thinking and foresight that he fulfilled all the dreams of his father, which Jamsetji could not fulfill during his life. With the help of his close relative R.D. Tata, he first focused on the projects his father had started. The first of these was the establishment of a modern iron and steel industry — the result of which is Tata Steel.

Along with that, with his increased morale he set up 'Tata Power' to supply electricity to the industries. These two are integral parts of the 'Tata Industry Group' today.

He served as a driving force for each member of his team. Whatever project he took up, he kept himself completely attached to it. He kept a close watch on every detail. He even travelled to mineral fields with scientists and explorers engaged in the discovery of cast iron.

The Tata group expanded significantly under the leadership of Dorabji. It expanded rapidly and diversified beyond Jamsetji's era to just three textile factories and the Taj Hotel. In addition to the largest steel company in the personal sector it soon managed and owned an integrated steel plant, three hydroelectric power companies, a large edible oil and soap factory, two cement factories. Apart from these, Indian Institute of Science, Bangalore was established during the tenure of Dorabji. In 1910, the King of England conferred him with the title of Knighthood (Sir). In this way he was appreciated and honoured for his works.

Dorabji had a great interest in sports. This attachment towards sports was further enhanced when he was studying in Cambridge. In order to increase interest and improve the level of sports in India, he started the 'Olympic Movement'. As the President of the Indian Olympic Association in 1924, he bore the expenses of the Indian batch participating in the Paris Olympics. He was also elected a member of the International Olympic Association.

❏❏

Lady Meherbai

Dorabji's wife Meherbai has a remarkable place in the India's women movement. She was always devoted towards the education and the welfare of Indian women. She was the founding member of the 'Bombay Presidency Women Council' and later the 'National Council of Women'. She agitated movements for giving higher education to women, abolition of purdah and eradication of untouchability. In this work she was fully supported by Dorabji also. She called a surveyor from England to conduct a survey of girls' education in India. The survey was continued for one year and came out in form of a book, which served as a pioneer for women education for the next several years.

Her speech about India and Indians at the Bottle Creek College, America was very compendious, covering every aspect of Indian life and society. Like Dorabji, she too was very fond of sports. She was a good tennis player and won many awards as well. Together they participated in many All India Championships and achieved success.

She was also an active member of the Indian Red Cross. During the war, she also worked hard in raising donations etc. In recognition of her contribution, King George V honoured her himself.

She died of leukemia on June 18, 1931. Dorabji established the 'Lady Tata Memorial Trust' in 1932 in her memory. This trust was formed to study various blood related diseases. In 1932, he established a trust fund, which was to be used for further work in research, disaster relief and other humanitarian purposes. The trust was named 'Sir Dorabji Tata Trust' and it is believed that he invested all his assets in this trust.

Dorabji also contributed greatly in the field of education. He gave a large amount of money to Cambridge University for a laboratory equipment. He also helped the 'Bhandarkar Oriental Research Institute' (Pune) financially to study Sanskrit.

He died on 3 June 1932 in Germany. His mausoleum remains near the tomb of his wife Meherbai in Brookwood Cemetery, England.

❏❏

Ratan Dadabhai Tata

Ratan Dadabhai Tata renowned as R.D. Tata was born in Navsari in 1856. It was here that he got his primary education. Later he received his higher education at Elphinstone College and then studied agricultural science in Madras.

After completing his education, he started his work with his father's company Tata & Co. When he started his work, the company's condition was not good, the business was heading towards recession. Hence, he was sent to Hong Kong for company work.

Even after his father's death in 1876, he continued to work. In 1883, he took over the charge of the company. The company was not in good state at that time. This was the time when he got an opportunity to demonstrate his financial ability and he got his company out of many problems and vicious circles.

Jamsetji was very impressed with the caliber of R.D. Tata. Therefore, in 1884, he made him a part of his company 'Empress Mills'. After this, in 1887, he was incorporated as a partner in his newly formed company, Tata and Sons.

Ratan Dadabhai was associated with its manager Bejanji Dadabhai Mehta in the 'Empress Mills'. Bejanji was then looking after the technical and management work, while Ratan Dadabhai was entrusted with the financial side. During the same period, he was entrusted with the task of opening a factory in Yavatmal along with his cousin, Dorabji Tata. The economic condition of the indigenous mill was not good at that time, hence its financial workload was assigned to R.D. Tata. Together with Dorabji under the guidance of Jamsetji, he successfully carried out his work and helped the company in overcoming difficulties.

The business of the company set up by Jamsetdji was different from that of Nausherwanji, so he gave the charge of the eastern branch to his cousin R.D. Tata. R.D. Tata moved to Hong Kong for a few years, where he set up branches in places like Shanghai, which ran the rice and silk business. This business flourished so much under his control that soon new branches opened in New York and Paris, which mainly traded in pearls and silk. It was in Paris that he fell in love with Suzanne Briere and in 1902 he married her.

After the death of Jamsetji, in 1907, the name of 'Tata and Sons' was changed to 'Tata Sons and Company'. It had three partners — Sir Dorabji, Sir Ratan Tata and R.D. Tata. The company operating from Hong Kong under the name of Tata & Co. was also merged with this new company.

R. D. Tata's main work was to look after business and financial work while staying in the Bombay headquarters. While staying here he played an important role in completing the projects - Iron and Steel Company, Hydroelectric Company and Indian Institute of Science, envisaged by Jamsetji. After the death of Sir Ratan Tata in 1918, R.D. Tata took over the important departments of the company. During the first world war when the company was going through a period of hardship, it was the work efficiency of R.D.Tata that helped the company overcome such a difficult time. This was possible only because of his mature experience and unparalleled guidance.

Despite serious economic difficulties, he was always devoted to welfare works and humanity.

He was also a member of the 'Imperial Legislative Council' for some time which later helped him in assuring the rescue of the iron and steel industry.

His visit to Japan in 1890 helped develop the India-Japan trade relationship. The Japanese emperor recognized his work and conferred him with the title 'Third Order of Rising Sun'. He departed for his heavenly abode on August 26, 1926.

❐❐

Sir Ratan Tata

Jamsetji's younger son Sir Ratan Tata was born on January 20, 1871. He was 12 years younger than his brother Dorabji. He completed his education from St. Xavier's College, Bombay. He got married to Nawazbai in 1892.

After marriage, Ratan started living in Esplanade House with his parents and wife. After the death of his father Jamsetji, he made Brightland his place of residence in the Marine Line. He later built a magnificent building for himself on Wodby Road, which was completed in 1915. He was able to stay in this building only for a few months, after which he went to England for his treatment and then took his last breath there only.

After the death of his father Jamsetji, started working in a French insurance company, whose agent in India was 'Tata and Sons'. He also handled the work of 'Tata and Company', which did business of textiles, yarn, silk, pearls and rice etc. It had branches in Paris, Shanghai, Kobe, New York and Rangoon.

Although Sir Ratan Tata was associated with the functioning of 'Tata and Sons', most of its responsibility was on his elder brother Dorabji. Ratan took special interest in land acquisition in Mahim and Bandra and later the government took up this task.

Sir Ratan Tata was socially very active. He had keen interest in travelling as well. In the latter part of his life, every year he used to spent much of his time in England. He was a member of the 'Carlton Club', London and was considered a respected member of the High Society of England. In 1906, he bought 'York House' in Twickenham, near London, England, and developed a beautiful garden in an area of 12 acres adjacent to it.

Social consciousness was also was one his qualities. He was fully aware of the importance of the struggle done under the leadership of Mahatma Gandhi against the excesses of the British in South Africa. Therefore, he not only gave it moral support but helped in financial terms as well. As a contribution to this struggle, he sent ₹ 1,25,000 to Gandhiji in five instalments. On the other hand, he gave adequate support and cooperation to the excellent work being done by Gopal Krishna Gokhale and his 'Servants of India Society' in the country. He also gave a total financial assistance of rupees 1,10,000 to this movement under his generous support.

Sir Ratan was very much agitated after seeing the poverty and plight of India and its people and he wanted to improve it. He urged that this matter should be investigated in a scientific manner. In 1912, he proposed financial assistance to the University of

London to set up a body to work in this direction, so that suggestions could be made for identifying and diagnosing the causes of poverty and poor conditions. It was formed in 1913 and Sir Ratan accepted to give aid for three years at the rate of 1,400 pounds per year. In 1916, it was extended for five years. Even after his death this payment was made by his trustees till 1931. Many candidates did their research in this area and presented papers as well.

Sir Ratan Tata also provided economic assistance to the London School of Economics to open its department for the study of 'Social Sciences'. This new department was called 'Ratan Tata Department of Social Sciences' in 1919. Later 'London School of Economics' took its complete charge and accordingly its name was also changed.

Sir Ratan Tata was also very interested in India's past. In 1912, he proposed to provide economic assistance for archaeological survey and excavation in Bihar and Odisha. Accordingly, extensive excavation in Pataliputra, was done under the supervision of Dr. A.B. Spooner. From 1913 to 1917, Sir Ratan Tata provided assistance of 75,000 rupees for this work. Many coins, terracotta items and other valuable materials were found in this excavation, which are still preserved in the Patna Museum.

Sir Ratan Tata was very kind hearted. He gave donations for any such work, which affected him. He contributed greatly for relief in the event of natural calamities like flood, famine or earthquake. Apart from this, he also provided financial assistance to public monuments, schools and hospitals. He financed

10,000 rupees per year for ten years to the 'George V Anti Tuberculosis League'. The institute operated by this institution used to treat poor patients of tuberculosis. In 1916, he was awarded the title of Knighthood (Sir) for his various service works.

He was also a great admirer of art. During his travels both at home and abroad, he used to collect photographs, oil paintings, guns, swords, silverware, manuscripts, characters and carpets, which were important in terms of art and education. Later he handed over the collection to the Prince of Wales Museum, Bombay.

In 1916, Sir Ratan visited China and Japan. He fell ill after his return. The doctors advised him to go to England for treatment. He left for England in October 1916 with his wife Nawazbai and Secretary P.P. Mistry. On the way, their ship fell victim to the torpedoes of the Germans. Although Ratanji was rescued along with all the other passengers, this delay on the way had an adverse effect on his health.

He died in September 1918 in St Abbs, Carnival. His mausoleum is in Brookwood Cemetery, London near to his father's mausoleum.

Sir Ratan Tata had no child. In his will, he devoted a considerable part of his wealth to philanthropic works.

◻◻

Lady Nawazbai

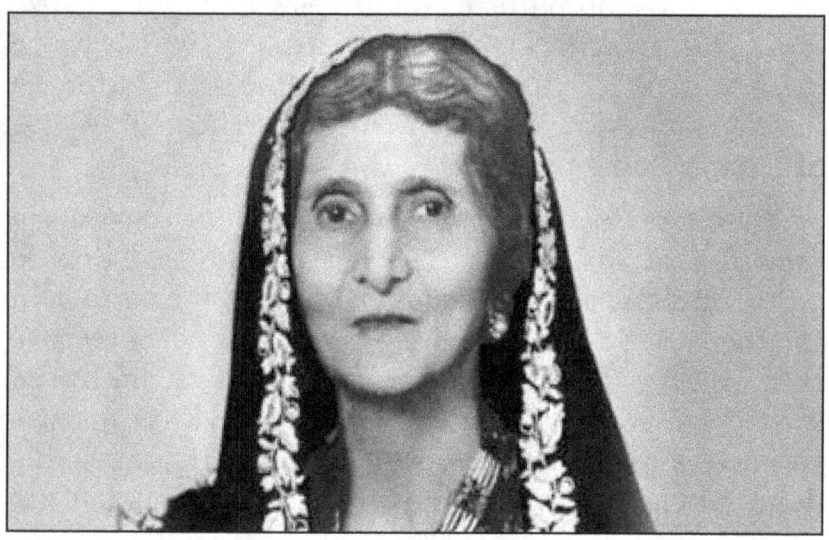

Nawazbai, the wife of Sir Ratan, was born in September 1877. She was married to Sir Ratan in 1890. She was proficient in horse riding and polo. They had spent a part of their lives in London and the couple was highly respected among the elite people. Like Sir Ratan Tata, Lady Nawazbai was also a great admirer of fine art. Her contribution in the collection of various artifacts cannot be underestimated. Nawazbai was widowed at the age of 41. She had a great responsibility to take care of the estate of Sir Ratan. She spent the rest of her life in a dignified way in the 'Tata House'.

After the untimely death of Sir Ratan, Nawazbai was inducted into the governing board of 'Tata Sons' in 1918. She held this position till her death. She died in August 1965. She was the first and only woman to be a member of the governing board of 'Tata Sons'. A generous donation to the 'National Metallurgical Research Institute' in Jamshedpur exemplifies her immense heart. By this, she demonstrated her willingness to spend the fund of Sir Ratan Tata Trust in creative work.

In 1928, she played a major role in the establishment of 'Ratan Tata Institute'. Through this, instead of giving cash assistance to the people, it worked towards providing necessary training and employment opportunities to the poor and needy people in individual institutions. She wished for the welfare of all. She was above the spirit of religion, sect and caste, therefore was ready to help everyone.

As Chairperson of the 'Sir Ratan Tata Trust', she invited S.J.I. Markham of the Carnage Trust to study the problems of the Parsi community and present a report on it. With this move, Parsi Charities organized themselves to make their 'charity' capable.

Childless Nawazbai wished for the survival of her husband's legacy, so she adopted Naval Hormusji Tata, son of Hormusji Tata. In this way, this adopted son of Lady Nawazbai later took over the work of the Tata family.

□□

Naval Hormusji Tata

Naval Hormusji Tata was born on 30 August, 1904 in Bombay to a middle-class family.

His father Hormusji Tata was a spinning master in a mill in Ahmedabad. His father died when he was just four years old. This was a great shock to his family. It was a difficult task for their widowed mother to raise her growing children. His relatives in Bombay brought them some relief. After that, their family house in Navsari became their shelter.

Eventually the family settled in Surat. Their necessary expenses started to be met from the income of Zardozi work being done by their mother.

Meanwhile, Dorabji arrived on the scene. With his help, two of Naval's brothers got shelter in the J.N. Petit Parsi orphanage. There were about 300 children in this orphanage, for whom a limited amount of money was available in the form of budget for food, clothes and health. It was more or less a difficult life.

Staying in this position, this child later went on to reach an important position at the Tata Institute. It was a unique blend of his determination and personal qualities that brought him to this milestone of success.

As it is well known that Jamsetji Tata was married to Heerabai. He had two sons - Dorabji and Ratanji, who had no heir. When he was growing up in an orphanage, he was adopted by Sir Ratan Tata's wife, Lady Nawazbai.

Sir Ratan Tata died in England in 1918 at the age of 47. At a meeting of family members chaired by Sir Dorabji, it was decided that a son is must for 'Utthama Sanskar', so one should be adopted as a son. Naval's mother was Sir Ratan's favourite cousin, so it was decided to adopt Naval. Nawazbai accepted this family decision and thus Naval Hormusji Tata was adopted. Nawazbai immediately wanted to take Naval out of the orphanage, but the rules of the orphanage came in the way. He was able to leave from there only when he passed his tenth examination while living there.

Although he suddenly became a member of an influential family in the country, but he never forgot his past. He used to say that I am thankful to God, who gave me the opportunity to experience the sufferings of poverty, which moulded my personality accordingly in the years to come.

After completing his Bachelor's in Economics from Bombay University, he went to England to complete a short course in accountancy. After returning from there in 1930, he entered the Tata organization as Dispatch Clerk Assistant Secretary.

He soon joined the post of Assistant Secretary at Tata Sons. In 1933, he was made Secretary in the Department of Aeronautics. He was later transferred to the textile department as an executive. Seeing his abilities, he was made Joint Managing Director of the textile factories operated by Tata in 1939. In 1941, he was promoted as a director in Tata Sons. In 1948, he took over as the managing director of Tata Oil Mills Company Limited. Prior to this, he had already become the chairman of Tata Mills. In the following years he was promoted swiftly. He was made the chairman of other textile factories and three electric companies and later was appointed vice-president at Tata Sons.

In this way, he had the direct responsibility of managing four textile mills, three power companies and the Sir Ratan Tata Trust. Apart from this, he was also responsible for guiding several other companies and trusts of the group.

Despite being surrounded by work engagements, he maintained his calm nature, goodwill and humility like qualities in his personality and never forgot his past.

Despite his busy schedule at Bombay House, he used to meet people of all sections of society. He was very fond of various trusts operated under the name Tata; because the work of these trusts was based on a spirit of philanthropy. Therefore, he felt a personal liability towards these works.

He was the President of the Indian Cancer Society for nearly 30 years. He also contributed greatly in the field of sports. He was also the President of the 'Indian Hockey Federation' from 1946 to 1961. He was the first chairman of the 'All India Council for Sports'. He also provided services to the 'International Hockey Federation'.

Despite a tiring lifestyle of the day, he kept himself fresh and was humorous as well. He was a very social and simple man. The employees also enjoyed his interesting jokes and respected him.

His work on labour relations was also much better than predecessors. He was an honest and open person. He had a keen interest in solving the problems of the working class. According to the situations, he used to put forward his views and considered all options adequately to solve a problem.

In 1946, he represented the Indian textile industry in the International Labour Union. His ideas were highly appreciated. In 1957, he was elected a member of the Regulatory Committee of the International

Trade Union and remained its member until his death in 1989. In 1966, he was elected as a member of the 'Labour Panel' of the Planning Commission in the country.

'The National Institute of Labour Management' was established by him, which is today known as the 'National Institute of Personal Management'. He was also its president from 1951 to 1980. He worked to bridge the growing gap between the owners and employees due to various reasons. He suggested fair and appropriate measures. He considered himself an advocate of employee interests and did continuous and remarkable work for their rights and interests. He also took full care of the interests of the employees of the unorganized sector.

He was the President of the Indian Hockey Federation for many years. During his presidential tenure, India won three consecutive Olympic gold medals in Olympic hockey. Tata Sports Club played an important role in serving the Indian hockey.

He was rich in an all-round talent. Many times, he was offering his services to several institutions simultaneously, such as Indian Institute of Science, Swadeshi League, Bombay State Social Welfare Council, National Safety Council etc. He was also the chairman of several public welfare trusts.

On Republic Day in 1969, the President honoured him with 'Padma Vibhushan'. In the same year he was honoured for his contribution to maintaining industrial peace.

Naval Hormusji Tata was married to Sunu. His household life was not pleasant. After the divorce of Naval and Sunu, Lady Nawazbai took over the responsibility of raising their sons Ratan and Jimmy.

On 5 May 1989, Naval Hormusji, of a simple heart and reformative tendency passed away. He was in favour of giving everyone equal opportunities for progress.

❑❑

J.R.D. Tata

Jahangir Ratan Dadabhai (J.R.D.) was born on July 29, 1904 in Paris. His mother was French. His father's name was Ratan Dadabhai Tata. He was known among people as Jamsetji's cousin and R.D. He did his education in France, Japan and other countries. He also served primary service in the French army for one year. He wished to remain in the army, but God had planned something else for him. So he had to say goodbye to the French army. He wanted to pursue engineering education from Cambridge University, but in the meantime, he received a message from his father to return to India and complied as an obedient son. Returning here, he found himself in an environment and business empire that he was not used to. His work started as an assistant at Tata Sons. Shortly after his father's death he was inducted as a director in the company in 1926. He was appointed chairman in 1938. J.R.D. was a charismatic person.

He contributed to the industrial development of India for almost 53 years. On 25 March 1991, he handed over the charge of Tata Sons to his junior partner Ratan Naval Tata. The board of Tata Sons unanimously elected him as its lifetime chairman (retired).

J.R.D. is considered the founder of civil aviation in India. He was the first pilot in India to achieve this qualification. In 1932, he founded India's first national carrier, Tata Airlines. In 1946, it was renamed as 'Air India Limited'. The inaugural flight of Tata Airlines travelled between Karachi to Bombay and was operated by J.R.D. himself. In the following years, he established Air India International Ltd. as a joint venture with the Government of India for long-haul international flights. He was its executive chairman until its nationalization in 1953.

On his suggestion, the Government of India set up two flying corporations—Air India and Indian Airlines, which were formed for international and domestic flights respectively. He was appointed the chairman of Air India. He continued working in this post till 1978.

At the age of 78, on the fiftieth anniversary of Indian Civil Aviation, he repeated his 1932 inaugural flight in a 50-year-old aircraft on 15 October 1982.

He was awarded several awards for his contribution to the aeronautical field. In 1948, he was awarded the rank of Honorary Group Captain in the Indian Air Force and in 1966 as Air Commodore (Honorary). Apart from this, he also received many international awards.

He took care of Tata Airlines like a child. He had worked hard in its imagery, from the outline to putting it on the practical plane and later in its development and care. This was the reason that he strongly opposed the nationalization of Air India by Jawaharlal Nehru in 1953. Nehru gave him the leeway to take control and management of the cargo planes, from where he was separated in 1977 by a law.

Operations of Air India were an example of J.R.D.'s excellent efficiency. The principles of socialism were then highly prevalent. Industries had to work under a variety of rules and restrictions, yet J.R.D. tried his best to lead the country on the path of industrial upliftment.

It is also clear from this that when J.R.D. took over the position of chairman of Tata Sons, then the Tata group had 14 companies under its control. In his nearly 50-year tenure, that is, until July 1988, there were 95 companies that were started or controlled by the Tata group. Under his mature leadership, the Tata group expanded in all directions. Prominent among them are electricity, engineering, hotels, consultancy services, information technology, consumer goods and other industrial products.

His contribution in the field of science and medicine is also unique. During his tenure, Tata Institute of Social Science, Tata Institute of Fundamental Research, National Institute of Advanced Sciences, Tata Memorial Hospital touched new heights in their respective fields.

J.R.D. gave a new direction to the current business practices at that time. Instead of adopting the practice of running an enterprise under the supervision of members of the households, they adopted a purely commercial approach. Bringing the talent forward, harnessing their skills and giving them an opportunity to grow. Some difficulties also came into his way, but he faced those challenges.

For J.R.D., the aim of national interest lied in the progress of the country and he made his full contribution in thus direction. The idea of donating at the simple level and having a sense of fulfilment of his duty was not acceptable to him, rather, he gave priority to such works which were sustainable and gave permanent results. Keeping this in mind, the multi-purpose 'Tata Trust' was established in 1944. J.R.D. established the 'Thelma Tata Trust' in Bombay with the proceeds from the sale of his shares. The aim of this trust was to improve the status of women of disadvantaged sections and to lead them towards progress.

He was an advocate of family planning and population control in the interest of the country. In recognition of his efforts, he was awarded the U.N. Population Award in September 1992. He was the founding member of 'Family Planning Institute'. He was also the Chairman of the Governing Body of the Tata Institute of Fundamental Research, Member of the Atomic Energy Commission, President of the Court of Indian Institute of Science, Bangalore. He served as chairman of the 'J.N. Tata Endowment for the Higher Education of Indians' and 'Homi Bhabha Fellowship Council.' Along with this, he handled the post of chairman of the Sir Dorabji Tata Trust, J.RD. Tata Trust and Jamsetji Trust.

He also received many national and international awards. Prominent among them were 'Padma Vibhushan', 'Legion of Honour' of France, 'Order of Merit of the Federal Republic of Germany' and doctoral degrees from Allahabad, Bombay, Roorkee and Banaras University etc. The Government of India honoured him with the 'Bharat Ratna', the highest civilian honour of the country in 1992. He died in Geneva in November 1993.

J.R.D. had met Thelma in France. Their romance with Thelma resulted in a happy marriage and they got married in 1930. He was childless, but he accepted it as God's will. Although, he is not among us but his legacy will always remain alive. The country will always remember him.

❏❏

Ratan Tata

Ratan Naval Tata was born in 1937 in Bombay in the rich and famous Tata family. He is the son of Sunu and Naval Hormusji Tata.

Ratan's childhood was a bit unfortunate as well. When he was just seven years old, his parents got divorced. Ratan and his brother Jimmy were raised by their grandmother Nawazbai. She had great affection for Ratan. Ratan Tata did his early education at Campion School in Bombay. At the age of fifteen, he was sent to the United States to pursue further studies. He received his bachelor's degree in Architecture and Structural Engineering in 1962 from Cornell University, USA. He also did a course in Advanced Management Program from Harvard Business School.

After coming to India in 1962, he entered the Tata group. At that time, J.R.D. was the chairman of the Tata group. He sent Ratan to Jamshedpur to work at Tata Steel, so that he could understand the work of Tata Steel properly. There he worked like the other employees only, wearing a blue uniform. It included all the work from removing the lime stones with the shovels to work related to the blazing furnaces.

In 1971, he was given the charge of National Radio and Electronics Company (NELCO). NELCO was going through economic difficulties at that time. Nobody expected its success. But looking at the future of Tata Company, Ratan succeeded in convincing the then chairman J.R.D. that more investment was needed in the company. Although, J.R.D. was not keen to invest more in it.

This was the time when the country was under the dominating influence of license and permit. As a result, he had to face many difficulties in carrying out his work. These difficulties gave him a new vision. Therefore, he focused on further improving his abilities and in 1975 received higher education in management from Harvard School. In December 1988, he was made the chairman of Telco. After the death of his father in 1989, he took over the charge of Sir Ratan Tata Trust as chairman.

During his tenure, J.R.D. Tata broadened the basis of Tata Sons. As a result, in 1980 where there were only 11 directors, by 1991 their number increased to 18. It included those people who played an important role in the development of the Tata Group. In later years, this kept changing.

On March 25, 1991, J.R.D. Tata proposed Ratan Naval Tata for the post of Chairman of Tata Sons as his successor and retired on his own.

❑❑

Tata Group's Journey Under the Leadership of Ratan Tata

When Ratan Tata took over the charge of the 104-year-old Tata Group, his predecessor, J.R.D. Tata had handled this work for almost 50 years. He gave the group a new shine, while on the other hand he also left an impression of his personal style. In the latter half of J.R.D.'s tenure, the powerful chairman and managing directors of various Tata Group institutions, which were closely associated with J.R.D., tried to leave their mark on the companies related to them in the backdrop of the closeness of their relationship.

In July 1991, the central government abolished many provisions of the M.R.T.P. and moved towards liberalization. This task of the government was quite a relief for Ratan Tata, who took charge just three months ago.

When Ratan Tata rose to the position of chairman, the operations of individual companies were in the hands of powerful chairmen or managing directors and they were operating in their own way. The main challenge for him was to bring them all together. He set the age of retirement for the post of chairman and managing director. This age was 75 years for the chairman and 65 years for the managing director. He organized the erstwhile companies, made sure to come out of some others, set up new companies and later acquired some. He made 32 new starts in the first decade of his tenure.

It was clear till the death of J.R.D. (1993), that Ratan Tata's attempt to organize the group companies under the banner of 'Tata Sons', had the blessing of J.R.D. with him. In this period of liberalization, the 'Tata' holding company gradually increased its share ratios in group companies such as Tisco (Tata Steel), Tata Chemicals, Telco (Tata Motors) and Tata Tea. Under him, Tata Consultancy Services was publicized. Meanwhile, Tata Motors was listed on the New York Stock Exchange.

In order to facilitate the operations, the Tata group sold its shares in the last decade of the century in a number of sectors such as edible oils (TOMCO), cosmetics (Lakme), pharmaceuticals (Rallis & Merind), paints (Goodlass Nerolac). In addition, he sold assets in ACC, computer and telecommunication hardware and oil. They split from joint ventures like IBM Timex.

Between 1990 and 2002, his main focus was on cars, telecom, insurance and fertilizers. Today, in the twenty-first century Tata Group's scope of work can be mainly divided into the following seven areas-

(a) **Materials:** such as steel and advanced plastics

(b) **Chemicals:** Inorganic fertilizers, pesticides

(c) **Engineering:** Automobiles, auto components, air conditioning

(d) **Energy:** Energy

(e) **Consumer goods:** Tea, coffee, watch

(f) **Services:** Hotel, retail, finance services, insurance, international trade

(g) **Information methods:** Software, industrial & telecom, automation & telecom

As soon as Ratan Tata took over as the chairman, he laid the foundation stone for many technology businesses and aimed at the development of many ventures. Under the efficient direction of J.R.D., he started giving form to his imaginations related to the Tata group. It was a transition period. With the beginning of liberalization, new beliefs and rules were being replaced in place of old beliefs and systems.

With the change in the central industrial policy, the government was also trying to remove all the discrepancies in the establishment of individual undertakings and to create a suitable environment for their development to some extent. As a result, some public sector domains were opened up to the private sector. The economy that was confined and shrunk under the cloak of socialism for around a

Tata Group's Journey Under the Leadership of Ratan Tata // 53

decade got the chance to spread. The economic policies of some countries had changed and this phase was continuing in many countries. In such a situation, the Government of India also understood that liberal policies are needed to achieve good economic growth.

Ratan Tata was also benefited from this new thinking and situation, as a result he made strides in many new areas of the industry. It is also worth mentioning here that the Tata Group's overseas emoluments grew significantly due to the 'Tata Consultancy Service'. It was established by Ratan Tata only in the 80s. Soon it became a well-known name in the consultancy sector on the world stage.

❑❑

Ratan Tata's Foresight

When Ratan Tata took over the command of Tata Sons, not only the Tata Group but the entire country was witnessing a change in the old trends. With the liberalization of the Indian economy and change in the thinking of the global economy a new era of opportunities and challenges was unfolded. He took many steps to meet these challenges and to convert the available opportunities into success.

To increase holdings in companies managed by Tata: With this thought, by 2002 the holding in Tata Steel increased from 8 to 26 percent, in Telco from 17 to 32 percent, in Voltas from 22 to 25 percent. In some other companies like Tata Chemicals, Tata Tea etc. it remained unchanged (30 percent). In some new companies the holdings were 76 percent in Tata Infotech, 26 percent in Trent Ltd. and 50 percent in Infomedia.

A Group Executive Office was established in the year 1998 as a part of the operation and consolidation of the Group's policies. In this a group chairman and 5 members, who were from group company, group finance, group human resources and new group project were included.

Later in 2002, Tata Group Corporate Centre was set up, with Group Executive Officers as members.

It included — Ratan Tata, Dr. J.J. Irani, R.K. Krishnakumar, M.A. Sunawala, R. Gopalakrishnan, Ishat Hussain and K.A. Chokar.

A code of conduct was prepared to use the name 'Tata'. If anyone disregards it, he had to stop using the name 'Tata'. The Tata model of business excellence was launched in 1994. Seeing the importance of the Tata brand, the Tata companies were expected to work for the further development of the brand name.

When Ratan Tata took over, his main challenge at that time was to bring companies under one framework so that they could work in one direction. He tightened his grip on companies. Although, to a larger extent the autonomy of the company was with him only, but he retained the right to submit his objection in the event of disagreement as a shareholder in major policy decisions and to bring it to a definite outcome.

Today, the Tata Group is not a loose association of different companies, but a closely connected group, which is headed in the direction to meet the challenges of the future.

❑❑

Strong Intention

Tata Chemicals and Telco were counted as two of the largest companies in India till 1980, but an untoward occurred with Telco in 2000-01. Overnight, the market for its products fell by 45 percent and the company incurred a loss of ₹ 500 crore. In fact, from 1993 to 1997, Telco sales had increased by ₹ 7,500 crore. The sales fell flat when ₹ 1,700 crore was spent on the company's Indica car project. In such a situation, a huge reduction in sales and loss of ₹ 500 crore was a big challenge for the company and its employees. It was a direct injury to the self-respect of the employees and officers. They unanimously decided that we have to overcome this situation. The fact was that only the employees and officers of the company could handle this situation well, because they knew where and what the problem is and what is the solution.

Ratan Tata, linked this sense of self-esteem of the employees successfully to the company's resurgence and made successful use of it. And in the third financial year itself, i.e. in the year 2002-03, the company reached a profit of ₹ 500 crore (pre-condition). This achievement was nothing short of a miracle under the erstwhile circumstances.

He gave a new edge to the company in the difficult situation. A task force was formed at a higher level. In no time, forty action teams were formed, with 230 operation managers working on the allocated work. All these teams were from Tata Motors and Consultant sources. These teams worked day and night, made the data available to the concerned departments and after that the suitability was examined from the operational point of view. The deficiencies were determined and work started accordingly.

The senior manager team met with many young employees and high-level executors from the chairman to the senior officials and got their views, took suggestions from them about the problems and appropriate steps were taken accordingly.

The second task was the use of special training programs and inspirational steps. For this, mixed groups of employees of all grades and management personnel of all levels were sent to workshops for training and motivation. The focus of higher leadership was to create a result-oriented work culture devoid of all kinds of shortages. It was this work culture that made impossible goals possible.

Tata Indica has been Ratan Tata's dream since 1993, which came true in 1999. Telco officials toured around the world to fulfill this dream. Actually, he wanted a car that suited the Indian situation. It should have the same space like the ambassador, Zen-like exterior design, Italian style and the French engine design. Ratan Tata had a mental connect with this project. So when he accepted the challenge, he worked hard for the success in that proportion only.

When it became necessary, he received expertise from all the possible sources. But developed it on its own. Hence, it was truly a national achievement.

As a result, when Indica came out of the showroom in 1999, the company had 1,15,000 bookings in which the entire amount was paid in advance. From this only its fame can be guessed. Later on, many improvements were made and many other models like Indica V2, Indigo, Indica Sedan etc. were developed.

Rovers in England needed a world class car in the same segment. Hence, it tied up with Telco to sell the Indica V2 in England and the European continent, and in five years a total of 100,000 cars were to be sold as City Rover. Its first batch was sent in 2003.

Tata Chemical was a leading company in its field in the pre-liberalization era of India. In 1990 it made three new beginnings. They were — Babrala Fertilizer Plant in Uttar Pradesh, the establishment of Tata Kisan Kendra and production of branded edible salt. Out of these, Babrala plant was started in 1994. Urea was to be produced in it. Along with this, an ammonia plant was also established in the same complex. Babrala Complex had set new records in the fields of production, technology, energy conservation and safety.

Despite this, in the year 1999, an odd situation arose due to heavy arrival of soda ash from China and reduction in fixed rate of urea. For the first time in the company's history, it had to declare a loss for the quarter that ended in June 2000.

As a result, a new management committee was formed. Working under Prasad Menon, the committee had to earn the company from afresh by refocusing the factors responsible for company's position. It took some important steps of different nature. These steps had the desired effect and in 2001-02 the amount of profit reached ₹ 200 crore.

It was Ratan Tata's foresight that helped to take all the necessary steps to deal with an imminent threat, and Tata Chemicals not only returned to its track but also started to gallop.

Tata Steel was in strict need of renewal to remain in competition during the period of liberalization and this renovation required retrenchment of about 35,000 employees. At that time, both the factories and mines of Tata Steel had a total of 78,000 employees. Everyone was aware of its immediate consequences of sorting on such a large scale, but sorting was equally necessary. After the estimation of profit and loss was made under Ratan Tata's leadership, it was concluded that this problem can be solved easily if some attractive conditions are laid down for retrenchment of employees. The adverse effects from these conditions will be eliminated within a few years of modernization and eventually it is a profitable deal. The conditions for voluntary leave were so attractive that a large number of employees applied for voluntary leave and soon the company got rid of the additional employees. All this was achieved by maintaining great ease and industrial harmony. This is the reason why Tata Steel not only remained in competition in the coming years but also surpassed miles. Not only this, it was also able to acquire heavily competitive steel companies.

His strong intentions are also reflected in the Singur land acquisition dispute case, where he preferred to move away instead of succumbing to some people's stubbornness.

Some famous Tata Owned Companies and Brands

Tata Group is India's largest business group in terms of market order and revenue. Established as a multinational company, headquarters of this group is in Mumbai. It is recognized as a respected group all over the world. Its main areas of business are steel, automobiles, information technology, communication, energy, tea and hotels, etc. Its business is spread over 85 countries across 6 continents. Its products and services are exported to 80 countries of the world.

Engaged in 7 business sectors, this group is organized from 98 companies. Of these, 27 companies are listed as public companies. 65.8 percent of the Tata Group is owned by its charitable trusts. The largest share in the group is of Tata Steel, Corus Steel, Tata Motors, Tata Communications, Tata Consultancy Services, Tata Power, Tata Tea, Titan Industries, Tata Teleservices and Taj Hotels etc.

❑❑

Tata Steel

Founded on the belief of Tata, Tata Steel is the first steel plant not only in India but also in Asia. Tata Steel has created a new history by acquiring the Anglo-Dutch steel company Corus. This is the largest acquisition by an Indian company abroad and is in keeping with Tata Steel's reputation.

Jamsetji struggled hard to establish a steel plant, but he died three years before the site was sought. Before his death, he made sure that his dream came true. Members of the team that fulfilled his dream were- his son Dorabji Tata, expert surveyor C.M. Weld and Shapurji Saklatwala and Charles Page Perrin, Consulting Engineers, and Jamsetji himself went to New York to invite them.

Perrin prepared a detailed project report of the company's plant. Even after submitting the report, Charles Perrin stayed in India until the decision to establish the plant at Sakchi was made. Sakchi's name was later changed to Jamshedpur and this conversion of name was done by Lord Chelmsford, the then Viceroy of India. Only then the Kalimati station got the name 'Tata Nagar'.

In those days, the spirit of Swadeshi was in spate. Based on this sentiment, Tata Iron and Steel Company turned towards the Indian capital market and on August 26, 1907, issued shares for sale.

Investment letters were received from 8,000 Indian investors in just three weeks. The Maharaja of Gwalior purchased the entire 40,000-pound debenture issued for the availability of working capital. 2.32 crore was raised by issuing common, primary and deferred shares, through which a steel plant of 72,000 tonnes annual production capacity was to be set up. Installation of the plant started in 1908 and the first body was produced in February 1912. Tata had 11 percent stake in this company.

More than once, it was threatened with its takeover by the government. To prevent this possibility, a bill was introduced in the Central Legislative Assembly in 1924. This idea was fueled for the second time during the Janata Party rule (1977–79) in 1977 by the then Minister of Industry, but nothing happened.

Jamsetji dreamed of doing something by setting up Tata Steel. Tata Steel's dream was fulfilled Dorabji and J.R.D. Tata. But J.R.D. Tata was the person who increased Tata's assets from 62 crore to 10,000 crore in 1990. J.R.D. had the natural talent of testing man and developing leadership. He went on to help an outstanding manager like Russi Mody to excel and later rose him to a prestigious position. Mody improved the marketing operations and formed the Export Cell. He founded the 'G Blast Furnace', which according to the 2004 national record was the largest 'blast furnace' of Tata Steel.

J.R.D. Tata's successor Ratan Tata took over the charge of the steel company from Russi Mody in 1992. The company's competition was mainly about prices due to the liberalized Indian economy. Therefore, Tata Steel was not in good condition at that time. McKinsey report in the late 1990s advised Tata Steel to opt out of the steel business. But the real scene proved to be an eye opener. Successional changes were made in the company. Through advanced and attractive schemes, the company got rid of the excess of employees and the number of employees decreased from 78,000 to 43,000. This goal was achieved without harming the industrial harmony. The company distanced itself from many non-core businesses. The main thrust was to maintain the quality of steel as well as cost reduction and to bring prices to competitive levels using advanced technology. Meanwhile, a cold rolling mill was established. In 2001, B. Muthuraman replaced J.J. Irani as Managing Director of the company. Despite steep fluctuations in steel prices in 2001-02, Tata Steel was among the five steel companies in the world that made a profit. In the subsequent years, significant success was recorded through branded products and retail.

The company made several acquisitions over the past few years. Among these, the acquisition of Corus Steel is a historic event.

The company, which was earlier ranked 56th in steel production, has become the sixth largest steel producer in the world on its 100th year, it also grew significantly in the following years.

❏❏

Tata Chemicals

Tata Chemicals was established in 1939. Its first consignment of imported turbo generators from a foreign manufacturer were ruined due to the ongoing World War II and sank into the sea. After this, its next shipment somehow reached Bombay. But the company's early years were not good. The company had to face many difficulties from installation to production. Its most profitable business would have been the production of soda ash, but at that time only 6 companies of the world had the technology to produce it. But Tata Chemicals prepared its formula on its own. The second task was to produce at least 400 tonnes daily. Darbari Seth, a Chemical Engineer, laid the entire outline of the chemical plant in front of J.R.D. Agreeing with him J.R.D. handed over the responsibility of engineering, fabrication and installation of new machines at Mithapur to him.

Darbari Seth and his team completed the work of installation by working day and night and at the same time ensured that they all worked together. As soon as the plant was ready, the target of producing

400 tons per day was also handed over to the same team. Within the first fortnight, production from the plant reached 545 tonnes per day.

Today Tata Chemicals Ltd. Is the second largest soda ash producer in the world. Other than India, its production units are in other countries like UK, Kenya and USA.

Apart from this, the company also produces sodium bicarbonate, sulphuric acid, sodium tripoli phosphate on a large scale. Apart from this, Tata Chemicals Ltd. (TCL) is the largest producer of urea and phosphate fertilizers in India. Not only this, it is also the largest producer of branded iodized salt in India.

In 2003, Tata Chemicals gained control of Hindustan Lever Chemicals, the leader in the phosphate category in West Bengal, Bihar and Jharkhand. Hindustan Lever Chemicals factory is in Haldia and Tata Chemicals factories are in Mithapur (Gujarat) and Babrala (UP). A plant for its nitrogen fertilizer production in Babrala was also in progress. Tata Chemicals has introduced a number of branded productions over the years due to its large and diverse dealer network and has made good inroads through farmer training programs.

Tata Kisan Kendras have done revolutionary work in this direction. Tata Chemicals also exports 10-15 percent of its products.

□□

Tata Motors

Tata Motors is the largest automobile company in India. According to estimates in 2007-08, its revenue was ₹ 35,651 crore. It ranks highest in India in production in each category of commercial vehicles. As far as passenger vehicles are concerned, it is counted among the top three manufacturers. The company ranks fourth in truck production and second in bus production. Thus, it is a well-known name in the field of automobiles worldwide.

Telco (currently Tata Motors) was founded in 1945 and started production of vehicles in 1954. Today more than 40 lakh Tata vehicles are running on the roads of India and they have entered every corner of the country. Tata Motors' manufacturing units are located in Jamshedpur, Pune, Lucknow and Pantnagar (Uttarakhand).

In 1998, after many years of hard work and research Ratan Tata launched the first Indian car known as Indica. Cars under its brand are Indigo and many other names were subsequently produced and exported to many countries. In 2004, Tata Motors acquired the Daewoo Commercial Vehicle Company of South

Korea. It was the second largest truck manufacturer in South Korea. In this way, the restructured Tata Daewoo Commercial Vehicle Company launched several new vehicles in the Korean market and also started exporting them to other countries. In 2006, Tata Motors launched a mini truck in the market. It was quite successful and is in great demand in the market. As a result, its production has reached above 2,50,000 annually today.

In 2005, under a joint venture with Fiat, it has set up a new unit in Maharashtra to produce Fiat cars as well as Fiat powertrans and Tata cars.

The company is setting up new units at Dharwad in Karnataka and Sanand in Gujarat. The company has a network of around 3,500 centres for dealerships, sales & service and spare parts. It is also a distributor in the country of Fiat brand cars.

It also operates businesses in England, Thailand, South Korea and Spain through subsidiaries companies and ancillary units. These include the acquisition and operation of two well-known British brands Jaguar and Land Rover in 2008.

Earlier in 2006, Tata Motors formed a joint venture with Brazil's Marcopolo, which is world-renowned in the construction of buses and coaches, which will produce fully manufactured buses and coaches for export to the Indian market and other countries. In the same year the company became associated as a joint venture with the Thonburi Automotive Assembly Plant Company of Thailand, so that the company could produce and market the van for supply in Thailand. In 2008, the production of trucks called

'Xenon pickup trucks' had started at the Tata plant in Thailand.

Company had made a good place in the international market as well. Company's commercial and passenger vehicles are being marketed in many countries of Europe, Middle-East Asia, South-East Asia, South Asia, Africa and South America. Its joint ventures or franchises are working in Bangladesh, Ukraine, Kenya, Senegal and Russia.

The most important factor in the growth of the company in the last fifty years is - customer's need and satisfaction. For this there has been a tradition of research and development. 2,500 scientists and engineers of the company's Engineering Research Centre established in the year 1966, have made specific cooperation in the form of latest technologies and products for the use of the company. Apart from Pune, Jamshedpur, Lucknow in India, the research and development (R&D) centres of the company are working abroad in South Korea, Spain and England.

Tata Motors made the first light commercial vehicle in India and the Indigenous passenger car Indica in 1998. It made significant inroads in the Indian market within its journey of two years only.

In January 2008, Tata Motors showcased the Nano, an affordable price car. This was in keeping with Ratan Tata's promise that he made with his countrymen promising an excellent low-cost car. It was named the 'people's car'. It was a laud effort for the world automobile industry. Nano is a car that fulfils the dream of a comfortable and safe journey for millions of families within their purchasing capacity.

It is available in both standard and deluxe classes, in India. In the standard category, it has been priced at ₹ 1 lakh (excluding VAT and traffic expenses). That is why people have named it 'Lakhtakiya Car'.

This car has been built by assessing the needs of a common family. Accordingly, it has a relatively spacious passenger compartment, so that one can sit and spread legs easily. It is spacious enough for 4 passengers. It has an outstanding standard of regulatory safety standards required in India. Even in terms of pollution standards, it will emit much less pollution than all the two-wheeler being built in India. Keeping its weight light helped maximize performance by the energy consumed per unit. Due to high efficiency in energy consumption, the emission of carbon dioxide is also significantly reduced. Overall, this car is designed to be very useful for a small family.

Tata Motors can pave the way for an automobile revolution in the market by building many new advanced vehicles, in the coming years. All these vehicles will be technologically advanced and manufactured according to customer needs. These will use environment friendly technologies and energy. The Research and Development department of Tata Motors strives for this overall.

Tata Motors is also engaged in engineering and automotive solutions through its ancillary units. Apart from this, it is also involved in manufacturing construction equipment, vehicle parts, machine tools and factory automation solutions, and manufacturing and service operation of automotive and computer applications parts.

Tata Motors is also conscious of its social commitments. It is a signatory to the United Nations' Global Compact and is engaged in community and labour-oriented social work in accordance with its principles.

Accordingly, it is working in harmony with the welfare works and community development for the welfare of the rural population around its production units.

❑❑

Tata Tea

Tata Tea is the second largest tea company in the world, with a branded tea business spanning over 60 countries. The major companies in the Tata Tea Group are Tata Tea, the Tetley Tea Company of England acquired by Tata (this acquisition was made possible in 2004 at a cost of $ 407 million) and Tata Coffee.

The Tata Tea Group, established in 1964 as a joint venture with England's James & Finlay, is today trading in branded tea, coffee and other beverages. It also has its own tea gardens. While the Tata brand is at the top in India, the Tetley brand is the second largest 'tea bag' brand in the world. Apart from this, it also has its partnership in South Africa's 'Joekels Tea Packers' and the Polish tea brand 'Vitax and Flosana'.

Business Sector

Branded Tea- Tata Tea has five major brands in the country such as Tata Tea, Tetley, Chakra Gold,

Kanan Devan and Gemini with access to all major segments of the consumer. Its distribution network extends to about 12 lakh retailers.

- **Instant Tea:** Tata Tetley's export unit exports several types of instant tea powder to the US.
- **Speciality Tea:** Tata Tea sells black, green and herbal teas under the brand names Tetley, Gemka and Good Earth.
- **Coffee:** Tata Coffee produces 9,000 tonnes of coffee annually. Tata's 'Eight O' Clock' coffee brand is the third largest coffee brand in America.
- **Tea gardens:** Tata Tea Company has around 50 tea gardens across India and also has a stake in certain plantations in Sri Lanka.

Apart from these, the company also deals in energy drinks, 'Himalayan' brand mineral water. The joint ventures and ancillaries of Tata Tea are as follows-

- **Tata Coffee:** Formerly known as Consolidated Coffee, it is an ancillary unit of Tata Tea. Apart from this, Tata Tea also controls America's third largest coffee brand 'Eight O' Clock'.
- **Tata Tea:** The England-based Tetley Group's business spans the globe. It was acquired by Tata Tea in 2000.

Tata Tetley is an ancillary unit of Tata Tea, which deals with instant tea powder and exports it to the US.

Tata Tea Incorporation is a Florida-based ancillary unit of Tata Tea which supplies the bulk of instant tea powder to manufacturers.

Apart from this, Tata Tea is also associated with Mount Everest Mineral Water Company, which produces Himalayan brand mineral water. Tata Tea also has a stake in Sri Lanka's 'Watawala Plantations'.

Tata Tea produces and manufactures black tea through 18 tea gardens, in Kerala. This production and manufacturing is done through the 'Kanan Devan Hills Plantations Company'.

Recently, Tata Tea has entered into a joint venture agreement with China's 'Zhejiang Tea Import and Export Company' which will manufacture polyphenols and instant tea extracts.

◻◻

Tata Power

'Tata Hydroelectric Power Supply Company' was established in 1911. The Andhra Valley Power Supply Company, established in 1916, was then integrated with it.  Today, Tata Power Company Ltd. is India's largest private power generating company and has a power generation capacity of 2,300 Mega Watt. The idea of setting up some new units is underway and its production capacity is likely to increase significantly over the next few years. Tata Power is working not only in the field of hydroelectricity, but also in solar and wind power generation. As a personal effort in the field of power generation in India, the first attempt was made by Tata Power in 1915 at Bhivpuri and Khopoli plants. The company's thermal power plants are operating at Trombay in Mumbai, Belgaum in Karnataka and Jojobera in Jharkhand. Hydroelectric power plants are functioning in Western Ghats and solar energy power plants in Ahmednagar.

The company is a pioneer in the introduction and operation of excellent energy technology. India's first 500 MW unit was set up at Trombay by Tata Power only. The company's line and distribution losses are the lowest at 2.4 percent across India. For the last 90 years, Tata Power has provided excellent service to the power consumers in Bombay. A distribution unit of the company is presently functioning in Delhi as well. Established in a joint venture with the Delhi government, it is known as 'North Delhi Power Ltd.' (NDPL). This venture has been very successful. Initially, the agreement between the Delhi government and Tata Power was for 5 years, that was to be reviewed in 2005. According to the sources, it was later extended for the next 4 years. In these 5 years, the line and distribution losses of the related fields have come down from 51 percent to 28 percent.

Tata Power Ltd. has implemented many projects in Middle-East, Africa and South-East Asia. These include the installation of various Mega Watt projects in Dubai, Saudi Arabia, Kuwait, United Arab Emirates, Iran, etc.

Tata Power as a joint venture with Power Grid of India has agreed to partnership in the 1200 km Taal Transmission Project. This is India's first transmission project which is based on government and private partnership.

Tata Power also obtained the contract to set up a 4,000 Mega Watt power plant at Mundra.

❑❑

Tata Consultancy Services

In the wake of the impending crisis of Monopoly Trade Restrictions (MRTP) in 1968, Tata Sons formed consultancy units on the basis of expertise. These were:

I. Tata Consultancy Services
II. Tata Consulting Engineers
III. Tata Economic Consultancy Services
IV. Tata Financial Services

After some initial strife Tata entrusted the responsibility to Faqir Chand, an outstanding electrical engineer, who was famous not only India but also in other countries due to his research papers and the discovery of excellent technology. For 1973-74 (two years) he was elected as one of the 30 members of the governing body of the American Institute that had membership of 3 lakh electric engineers. He also got an opportunity to visit many renowned institutions of America and see the research work going on there, as well as to know the views of his various colleagues.

He could well understand the upcoming information revolution and underlined India's bright future in the field of computers. He transformed Tata Consultancy Services (TCS) into a first level software engineering and service-provider. TCS was the one that developed the PAN (PAN) number for taxpayers for the Income Tax Department.

Today TCS has more than 1,12,000 IT consultants in about 50 countries of the world. Tata Consultancy Services is primarily in practice in the fields of IT services, business solutions and outsourcing.

Business Sector

Tata Consultancy Services has experience and expertise in many industries and service sectors. These include banking, financial services, health services, insurance, travel, traffic and hospitality services (hotels etc.), retail, energy, utilities, communication services, etc. It handles:

- **IT Services:** System Integration Solution, application development, testing solutions and management services.
- **Outsourcing:** Providing services and programs that help in efficient work, business solutions and management of services.
- **Business solution:** Providing a strategy and solution that helps customers overcome their business-management challenge.
- **Advisory Services:** Setting business goals, designing strategies, implementing suggestions and assessing their effectiveness.
- **Engineering and Industrial Services:**

Introducing solutions to companies in manufacturing sectors such as automotive, aerospace, industrial machinery, utility and pharmaceutical, etc., so that they can achieve engineering excellence and effective operations.

♦ **IT Infrastructure Services:** Providing services like- IT services, data centre management, End-user computing services, application management services, command centre services and management security services.

Apart from these TCS is also working in some other service sectors like business process outsourcing, enterprise solutions, full services etc.

TCS is also involved in the field of innovation with full vigour. It has excellent laboratories for acquiring advanced technology, which are working to research and obtain new products in new technology area. This includes new generation software processes, human-computer interfaces, nanotechnology, grid computing and more.

The joint, subsidiary and ancillary undertakings of TCS are as follows:

Direct Ancillary

♦ A. P. Online
♦ C. S. Technology
♦ C. M. C.
♦ Diligenta
♦ Exgenics Canada Incorporation

- Tata America International Corporation
- TCS Asia Pacific
- TCS Belgium S. A.
- TCS Deutschland GmBH
- TCS France S. A.
- TCS Netherlands B. V.
- TCS Sverige A. B.
- TCS Switzerland
- Tata Infotech, Singapore
- Tata Infotech, Deutschland GmBH
- TCS F. N. S.
- TCS Iberoamerica S. A.
- W. T. I. Advanced Technology
- Indirect Ancillary
- C.M.C. America Incorporation
- Swedish Indian I.T. Resources A.B.
- TCS Solution Centre S.
- TCS Argentina S.
- TCS Brazil S./C.
- TCS De Mexico S.A., De C.V.
- TCS Inversiones, Chile
- TCS De Espana
- TCS Brazil
- TCS Chile S. A.
- TCS Italia S.R.L.

- TCS Japan
- TCS Malaysia Sdn Bhd
- TCS Luxemberg S.A. Capellen
- TCS Portugal Unipessoal
- TCS Chile
- Comicrom S.A.
- Sisteco S.A.
- Sischrome S.A.
- Pentacomp S.A.
- Pentacomp Services S.A.
- Custodia De Documentos Intres
- Financial Network Services- From centers of Europe, Malaysia, Africa, Chile, and other countries
- Chang Won Investments, etc.

Headquarters of TCS is in Mumbai and it has a business spanning around 50 countries in the world. It has a training institute in Thiruvananthapuram and another institute called Data Research Development and Design Centre in Pune.

Despite the ongoing slowdown in the economic sector and the weak global industrial situation, the net profit of the company registered a growth of 19 percent as per the data released for the first quarter of 2009-10. Compared to the same period last year, the company's revenue grew by 12 per cent which is ₹ 7,207 crore.

Tata Teleservices

Tata's services continue to serve in each sector of teleservices, be it basic telephones, cellular telephone or internet or long-distance conversations  at national and international levels. International calls are executed through Videsh Sanchar Nigam Limited acquired by Tata teleservices.

Tata's engagement with the high-tech and services sector began in 1980 after Ratan Tata prepared a roadmap for entry into the sector. At that time this sector was safe for the Department of Telecommunications (DOT). The government's attitude was not firm. Tata opened up a joint venture with the Government of Kerala when the field of manufacturing of telephone equipment was opened to the private sector. Thus, Keltron was born. Tata in collaboration with a Japanese company started manufacturing PABX sets in Ahmedabad. It later contacted an American company.

In 1990, the government was ready to set up joint ventures with multinationals.

In 1995, the government invited tenders for cellular telephones in the country. Tata established a joint venture with Bell, Canada in 1997. In 1999, Tata Teleservices obtained a license to provide basic telecom services in Andhra Pradesh. Later, the company also obtained license to work in 5 other telecom circles — Karnataka, Tamil Nadu, Delhi, Gujarat, Maharashtra. These regions represent 56 percent of the country's customers.

TTCL with its ancillary unit Tata Tele Services (Maharashtra) is serving 32 million customers in 7,500 cities and towns across the country.

In 2005, the company forayed into the mobile services sector and operates its services in 22 telecom circles in the country. Its network is considered the best in India.

Business Sector

Tata Teleservices represents the Tata group in the field of telecommunications. This occupies a leading position in the field of CDMA 1x technology, in India. The company provides services in all areas of telecommunications, be it mobile services or wireless desktop phones or public booth telephones or wireline services. Its other services are value added services like voice portal, roaming, post-paid internet services, three-way conferencing, group calling, Wi-Fi internet, tata cords, calling cords services etc. Other products made available by the company include prepaid wireless desktop phones, public phone booths, mobile handsets, voice and data services such as games, voice portals, picture messaging, news, cricket, astrology and more.

The company along with Tata Teleservices Maharashtra is on the path to provide GSM services, which the company has planned to launch this year. Tata Indicom is playing a leading role in providing mobile services. The company has partnered with leading telecom service providers for reliable and technologically advanced networks.

Joint Ventures, Ancillary and Subsidiaries

- Tata Teleservices (Maharashtra)
- Virgin Mobile India, based on a franchise with Virgin Mobile Group. The company is headquartered in Mumbai.

Tata Communications

Tata Communications Ltd. (Formerly VSNL) international long distance, enterprise data, internet services is the largest telecom company in India.  This Mumbai-based company operates in about 80 cities in 40 countries. It is the world's largest submarine cable bandwidth provider through its ancillary Tyco Global Network. Another ancillary of Tata Communications is—VSNL, Canada, formerly called 'Teleglobe', a major partner of Neotel, South Africa.

Videsh Sanchar Nigam Limited was established in the year 1986 as a company owned by the Government of India. In 2000, the Tata group took over the possession of its control. In 2008, it was called Tata Communications Ltd. and it announced a global expansion program worth 2 Billion US $.

❏❏

Tata Sky

It is a joint venture of Tata Group and Star T.V., where Tata Group holds 80 percent stakes while the latter holds 20 percent stakes. Although it was established only in 2004, it started functioning practically from 2006. It is currently providing programs on around 140 channels. The company uses the Sky brand of Sky Broadcasting Company of England. In 2008, company announces to introduce the P.V.R. services under the banner of Tata Sky Plus, which will feature 45 hours of recording in MPEG-4 relative set top boxes.

❑❑

Titan Industries

It is a joint venture between Tata Group and Tamil Nadu Industrial Development Corporation. It is the sixth largest company in the world, which manufactures wrist watches. Watches manufactured by it include Titan, Fastrack, Sonata, Nebula and Xylys brands. Its repertoire includes watches, their accessories and jewellery etc. Its manufacturing units are in Hosur, Dehradun and Goa. It also manufactures jewellery under the brand name 'Tanishq'.

Titan's watch division was started in 1987. At that time, it was the third largest watch manufacturer in the country after H.M.T. and Allwyn. Titan watches occupy 25 percent of the market in India. It also exports watches to about 40 countries in the world through its marketing ancillary units. These ancillary units are in Singapore, Aden, Dubai and London. It has a long retail chain for marketing in the Indian market.

Tanishq

Currently, Tanishq is the most prominent jewellery brand in India. It is the first brand to offer branded jewellery in India. Adorned with 22 carats pure gold jewellery, diamonds or coloured 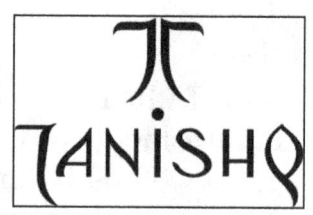 gems, it offers a wide range in the country. Tanishq was founded in 1995. It introduced new rules in the field of precious jewellery, challenging the dynastic tradition of goldsmiths. It caused excitement by entering the market with the guarantee of purity of Tata. Only then was it found that in India, jewellery manufacturers in the name of pure gold have been fooling the general public for centuries. It made the people aware with about the prevalence of rampant corruption through its criterion of technology in the purity based on personal belief. It was the brand Tanishq, which used an advanced technique such as karat meter to provide a means of testing the purity of gold without harming the gold jewellery.

Tanishq established a production centre and base of new research in the field of jewellery making in India. Spread over an area of 1,35,000 sq ft, its large unit is equipped with all modern machines and equipment. The factory set up at Hosur in Tamil Nadu centralizes the work of artisans making various styles of jewellery. On the one hand, they are artisans who are exploited by jewellery makers by making them work on less wages, while Tanishq's artisans are getting excellent working conditions and reasonable salary and other facilities. This is the reason why Tanishq is in great progress today and its marketing branches have opened in many cities.

◻◻

Tata Technologies

Tata Technologies is a Tata group company that works in the automotive industry and provides engineering and design solutions. In 2005, the company took control of Incat, of Europe, a major company operating in the same area. The headquarters of Tata Technologies Ltd. is located near Pune. The company operates its operations in the US and Europe through its wholly owned ancillary units, which is in Detroit, Denver and London. The company is also doing business in Thailand.

❏❏

Voltas Limited

This Mumbai-based Tata company is primarily an engineering, air conditioning and refrigeration company. It is engaged in a large area of industries like heating, air conditioning, refrigeration, ventilation, electromechanical projects, machine tools, textile machinery, construction equipment, mining, water management etc.

❑❑

Tata A.I.G.

Tata AIG General is a joint venture between Tata Group and American International Group (AIG). This led to the combination of Tata Group's prominence and A.I.G. making its global presence (in the insurance and finance services sector) in India. The Tata group holds 74 percent stake in this venture and AIG holds 26 percent. Tata AIG's General Insurance Company started its business in India in 2001. It provides services in each sector of general insurance such as motor, home, accident and health, travel, energy, marine, property liability and many other specialized financial sectors.

AIG is the world's leading business group in the field of insurance and finance services. AIG Units are offering their services to commercial, institutional and individual customers. Apart from these, AIG It also ranks highest in the world in the fields of companies, retirement services, financial and asset management services. AIG is listed on the Stock Exchange of New York, Paris, Tokyo, and Switzerland.

❏❏

The Taj Group

Jamsetji Tata had four main plans in mind, which he wanted to fulfil in his lifetime. They were—steel, hydroelectric power, a research university, and a hotel compared to no other hotel in Asia. He wanted to build a world class hotel in Bombay. Only this wish of his could be fulfilled during his lifetime when the magnificent Taj Mahal Hotel was inaugurated in 1903 in Bombay. Today Taj is the synonym of hospitality. Taj is the best in the world in terms of customer satisfaction. The Taj Group has opened training centres for excellent training of its employees.

At the 'World Travel Ceremony' held in Kuala Lumpur (Malaysia), the Taj Mahal Hotel, Mumbai was unanimously declared the best hotel in the Asia-Pacific region by all travel agents in the world.

In Kerala, Taj has started a project called 'Green Tourism', where specialist Ayurvedic treatment is available in five hotels of Taj Group.

The Taj Mahal Palace and Tower, Mumbai have made history since its inauguration in 1903. Many

Maharajas, princes, presidents and other prominent personalities have received hospitality of the Taj.

The Taj is also an excellent specimen of architecture which offers a fascinating view of the Arabian Sea and the Gateway of India. Besides foreign crafts and techniques there is a lot of use of Indian crafts and artifacts in it.

As a result of additional construction, the number of rooms in the hotel doubled, in 1970. The tower wing was speculated by a noted American sculptor named Melton Bekker. Dale Keller, a Swiss designer from Hong Kong, was in charge of its interiors. Indian essence was kept alive in it by giving special touch like the Udaipur style relief panels, Tanjore style columns, Indian restaurants etc. In 1990, the rooms on the top four floors were modernized again.

For almost a century, the Taj Mahal Palace has become a kind of store house for a variety of paintings and artistic things from all over the world. These things are displayed in large numbers here.

Services

The Taj Mahal Palace & Tower has 565 rooms and 46 suites and its facilities are also of excellent standard. It also provides personal butler service for the Taj Club room and suites. These butlers play an important role as a guide and assistant here.

Hotel business services include wireless Internet and broadband Internet access, colour copiers, in-house conferencing, mobile, laptops and portable printers on rent; translation, interpreters and secretarial services are also available on rent; and multimedia computers are also available. Other services include 24-hour dining, baby-sitting, beauty salon, car hire, currency exchange, dry cleaning, florist, house doctor, laundry and travel services etc.

The Taj and the attack of 26/11: On November 26, 2008, two of the big hotels in Bombay were attacked by Pakistani terrorists, the Taj Mahal Palace and Tower Hotel was also one of them were the terrorists caused immense destruction. Overall, there was considerable loss of life and property. The 31 people who died here included the staff along with the guests. Till the time Mumbai was freed from the clutches of the terrorists after a siege of more than 59 hours, they had killed 183 people and wounded 239 people in 10 places in total.

Taj was in bad shape. Blood-soaked rooms and corridors, gunshot hole, grenades ravages, burnt interior. Many Taj employees, including guests and security personnel, also lost their lives. The Taj's general manager's wife and two children also died in the fire. But like the people of Mumbai, the Taj employees also did not lose courage and pledged to bring the Taj back to a dignified place.

Re-welcoming of guest in Taj: The Taj Mahal Palace Hotel reopened on December 21, 2008, twenty-four days after the terrorist attack, and guests began arriving. By December 21, booking was completed in all its restaurants. On the occasion of the reopening of the hotel, Ratan Tata remembered the guests and security personnel who lost their lives in the terrorist attack and also thanked the employees who wrote a new chapter by saving the lives of others risking their own life.

The Tree of Life: A memorial called 'The Tree of Life' was also released in memory of those who lost their lives in the hotel, in the attacks of 26/11. Based on this, the names of those 31 people were recorded, so that they can always be remembered. The basis of this monument is the artwork of Jaidev Baghel, which was installed near the steps of the 5th floor, where it was found unshaken by the terrorist attack in its former position.

After this terror attack, Taj established a fund to help not only the people who lost lives in the Taj Hotel but also the victim of other parts of the city and the families of the deceased.

In this terrorist attack, many employees of the army, police, fire service, hotel, guests and general people also lost their lives and many were injured. Well-wishers from India as well as from outside India sent their best wishes to restore the hotel and provide relief to the victims.

Taj Public Service Welfare Trust

In response, the Taj group set up the Taj Public Service Welfare Trust. Its main objective was to provide immediate relief to the victims of the attack and the relatives of the deceased, be it ordinary people, security forces personnel or Taj employees or people from other institutions suffering from terror. This trust will continue to serve the victims of violence, natural calamities and other maleficent events in the years to come.

Apart from India Hotels Company Ltd. Sir Dorabji Tata Trust, Sir Ratan Tata Trust also approved valuable initial contributions in it. Consent from the government was also considered for contributions from foreign donors.

A board of trustees was also formed for this, which included Sir Ratan Tata, N.A. Sunavala, A.P. Goyal, R.K. Krishnakumar, R.N. Bickson and A.K. Mukerjee.

Ratan Tata worked patiently in this difficult time of the terrorist attack; but he was very upset by the negligence of the state machinery, the lateness and the lack of coordination among government agencies. While expressing his thoughts on taking responsibility of taking care of his own self, people and the institutions himself, he expressed his dissatisfaction clear and well.

❑❑

Large Acquisitions of Tata Group Across the Sea

Since 2000, Tata Group companies have acquired many big companies abroad. Their account is as follows-

- **Year 2000:** England's tea company Tetley was acquired by Tata Tea. The acquisition was concluded for $ 43.2 million. The acquisition made Tata Tea the world's largest packaged tea company.

- **February 2004:** Tata Motors signed an agreement to acquire the commercial vehicle unit from South Korea's Daewoo Group. It costed $ 102 million.

- **August 2004:** Tata Steel Limited purchased the Steel Miller NatSteel Ltd. of Singapore for $286 million.

- **June 2005:** Tata Coffee bought America's 8 O' Clock coffee company from Gryphon Investors.

- **July 2005:** Telecom company Videsh Sanchar Nigam Limited (VSNL) purchased the Teleglobe International Holdings Ltd. of America for $ 239 million and Tyco International Global Under Sea fibre optic cable network unit for $ 13.0 million.

Large Acquisitions of Tata Group Across the Sea // 99

- **Year 2006:** Tata Tea bought 30 percent stake of American Water Firm Energy Brand Incorporation for $ 67.7 million and sold it to Coca-Cola within a year for $1.2 billion.

- **January 2007:** Tata Steel acquired Anglo-Dutch steel maker Corus Group for $ 12 billion. This was the largest acquisition by an Indian company abroad so far.

- **March 2007:** Tata Power bought two coal mines in Indonesia for $ 1.3 billion.

- **January 2008:** Tata Chemicals acquired the American soda ash manufacturing company, General Chemical Industrial Products Inc. for $1.01 billion.

- **March 26, 2008:** Tata Motors succeeded in acquiring the luxury brands Land Rover and Jaguar of the British company Ford Motors. The deal was concluded for US $ 2.3 billion.

In addition, in recent times Tata Advanced Systems has tied up with a US-based helicopter manufacturer, Sikorsky, to manufacture helicopters. Under this, 19-seater S-92 helicopters will be built. The agreement was concluded for $ 350 million. The helicopters will be available for delivery from 2010.

Some Important Achievements

Ratan Tata has amazing management capabilities. He knew the value of time and used to make decisions accordingly. He also had to face failures, but he did not lose courage. He learned the mantra to climb the steps of success through his failures.

Acquisition of Steel Company Corus

'Corus' emerged in 1999, when British Steel merged with its rival Dutch steel company Hoogovens. The Corus employed 47,300 employees, including 24,000 at its various sites in the UK—Port Talbot, Scunthorpe and Rotherham.

Over the past few years, there was a significant reduction in its profit due to increase in raw material prices and rise in energy expenditure both in UK and Netherlands. Therefore, it was forced to join an institute whose production cost was low. When the sale of the Corus Steel Plant was decided, the big companies of the steel sector came into the fray. Tata Steel of Ratan Tata was also one of them. But then it was not considered to be a strong buyer. All kinds of thoughts were in the air. The first was that Ratan

Tata is not a serious contender, the second was that the Corus purchase would prove to be a loss deal for him. But Ratan Tata kept quiet at that time. He had made up his mind on what has to be done. It was not in his nature to retreat after making decisions, no matter what the challenge is. The same happened in this case. In the acquisition of Corus, he got a huge challenge from the Brazilian firm CSN.

The deal between Corus and CSN would have produced the fifth largest steel company in the world, with an annual production of 24 million tonnes. This would allow Corus access to low-cost and high-quality cast iron, which was available at the Casa de Pedra mine of CSN. Along with this, it would also have access to the fast-emerging markets of South America.

Whether the deal was with Tata or CSN in both cases, the new company would become the fifth largest steel producer in the world and it went into foreign ownership only a decade after becoming the British steel company Corus.

The Tata group joined the acquisition movement with an offer of 455 pence per share. Along with Brazilian CSN, Russia's Severstal was also interested in its acquisition. The Corus Board put its bid at 4.3 billion pounds. Severstal later expressed his reluctance to take over, but CSN. raised its bid to 475 pence per share. Meanwhile, there was intense discussion between CSN and Corus on the issue that a proposal of 500 pence per share came from Tata, which proved to be a serious setback for both. Both were quite surprised, but C.S.N. but C.S.N. raised its bid to 515 pence per share.

Corus is Europe's second-largest steel producer, with 12 billion pounds of annual revenue, crude steel production of over 20 million tonnes, that is mainly produced in England and the Netherlands.

The Corus consists mainly of three operating divisions-Striped products, long products and distribution & building systems. It has its own network of global sales offices and service centres, employing approximately 42,000 people.

Corus is a major supplier in the world's developed market. Its goods are supplied to the manufacturing, automotive, packaging, mechanical and electrical engineering, metal goods and oil and gas sectors.

After the acquisition, Corus is now an ancillary of Tata Steel. Today Tata Steel has business in about 50 countries around the world, including Corus, Tata Steel, Thailand and Nat Steel Asia. Around 80,000 employees are employed for the Tata Steel Group in five continents of the world. The crude steel production capacity of the group is estimated at 28 million tonnes.

It is estimated that by 2011-12, the combined production capacity of Tata Steel and Corus will be 40 million tonnes and the total turnover will reach $ 32 billion. This acquisition is the largest acquisition by an Indian company abroad.

The bid for the acquisition lasted for eight rounds. Brazil's CSN made its final offer bid up to 603 pence per share. Tata Steel made the bid in its favour by offering 5 pence more i.e. 608 pence per share. Therefore, the last bet was in the name of Tata, which did not let its own and the country's head bow down and thus created a new history.

◻◻

Acquisition of Jaguar Land Rover

Jaguar, founded in 1922, is the world's leading luxury and sports car manufacturer. Land Rover has been working in this sector since 1948. Jaguar Land Rover is made up of two big British car brands. Its manufacturing units are located in England.

The company has over 16,000 employees, of which around 3,500 are engineers. It has manufacturing units in Whitley and Geydon, UK.

Three models of Jaguar- XF, XJ and XK, are manufactured at Birmingham plant and those of Land Rover-Defender, Discovery-3, Rover Sport, etc, are manufactured at Solihull.

This business is a great means for England to earn money. 78 percent of Land Rover cars are exported to 169 countries. On the other hand, 70 percent of Jaguars are exported to 63 countries. Importers and franchise sellers are resorted to for sale to customers.

On March 26, 2008, Tata Motors purchased the Jaguar Land Rover business from Ford Motor Company for US $ 2.3 billion. Many companies of the world were trying to buy these famous brands, but only Ratan Tata got success.

Ratan Tata himself was present at the Jaguar Land Rover headquarters in Gaydon at the post-acquisition transfer ceremony. Leading officers were present on behalf of the acquired company.

Speaking on the occasion, Ratan Tata said that this is a memorable moment for Tata Motors. Jaguar and Land Rover are the two big British brands, which have a global market and have substantial growth potential. Jaguar Land Rover team will have our full support. The company will continue to have its own personal identity. Similarly, it will continue to work in accordance with its previously targeted business objectives.

In the procurement regime, royalty-free continuous ownership of the intellectual property rights construction plant, two design centers in England and a global network of national sales companies, were given to the Jaguar Land Rover.

A long-term agreement has been signed for the supply of engines, stamping and spare parts to Jaguar Land Rover. Other areas of cooperation by Ford will be the availability of information technology, accounting and testing facilities. The two companies will continuously cooperate in the field of design and development. Ford Motor Company will continue to provide financial assistance to Jaguar Land Rover buyers and customers for a duration in the transition period.

The deal will provide an important opportunity for Tata Motors to establish a strong footprint in the international automobile sector. With this, Tata Motors which was earlier known only for manufacturing low-cost cars will be able to make a mark in the luxury car category.

The deal also came as a big relief for the Ford company, as a lot of money was being spent on the creation of these two luxurious brands and the expenditure was more than the income. On the other hand, it was not able to get sufficient customers. As a result, the company was incurring heavy losses for the last two-three years.

◻◻

Entry of Land Rover Cars in the Indian Market

Almost a year after the acquisition, Tata Motors launched the Jaguar Land Rover car in the Indian market in the last week of June 2009. The three cars of the Rover models—Discovery-3, Range Rover and Sport—can each cost between ₹ 65 lakh and ₹ 1 crore.

While introducing these luxury cars to Indian customers, Ratan Tata said that 'With this, Land Rover brand cars have entered India. Although it had entered here in the past years, but the relationship with the customers here was severed in a few years. 'Even after the acquisition by Tata, during the economic downturn, its sales fell by one-third as compared to earlier sales, during the last one year. Keeping this in mind, Ratan Tata said, 'Jaguar Land Rover could not be praised in times of economic recession, but they are excellent products with their superb production. After coming out of the recession, we can say that it was a difficult decision to take ownership of it. But as an Indian, I am proud to be the owner of these brands. We will definitely bring back their lost dignity'.

Several prominent officials including Jaguar Land

Rover Chief Executive Officer David Smith were present on this occasion in Mumbai. Jaguar Land Rover series can be compared to Mercedes-S, Audi-6, BMW-7, etc.

With the entry of Jaguar Land Rover, Tata Motors has become a company engaged in the business of expensive luxury cars as well as low-cost cars for the common people.

❑❑

Chairman of Tata Sons

1. Jamsetji Tata (Year 1887-1904)
2. Sir Dorabji Tata (Year 1904-1932)
3. Sir Nowroji Saklatwala (Year 1932-1938)
4. J.R.D. Tata (Year 1938-1991)
5. Ratan Naval Tata (Year 1991-2010)

❑❑

Tata Group: Some Facts

- **Founded:** In the year 1868, Owned by Tata Sons, Founded by Jamsetji Tata.
- **Promoter Companies:** Tata Sons and Tata Industries.
- **Headquarters:** Bombay House, 24 Homi Mody Street, Mumbai.
- **Business Sector:** Materials, Engineering, Energy, Chemicals and Consumer Products, Information Systems and Communications.
- **Revenue of Group:** $62.5 billion (Rs. 2,51,543 crore) (Source: Year 2007-08).
- **Profit:** $5.4 billion (Rs 21,578 crore).
- **Number of Share Holders:** More than 32 lakhs.
- **Number of Companies:** 96 operating companies.
- **Number of Employees:** 3,50,000 employees.
- **International Condition:** Businesses in about 80 countries of the world.
- **International Revenue:** 38.3 billion dollars. 61 percent of the group's total revenue.
- **Companies listed on the Bombay Stock Exchange:** 27 Companies.

- Companies listed on the New York Stock Exchange: Two- Tata Motors and Tata Communications.

Management Board

Ratan Naval Tata, Chairman Tata Sons.

Members of Group Corporate Centre

- N.A. Sunawala. Vice-Chairman, Tata Sons.
- J.J. Irani, Director, Tata Sons.
- R.K. Krishnakumar, Director, Tata Sons.
- R. Gopalkrishnan, Executive Director, Tata Sons.
- Ishaat Hussain, Finance & Executive Director, Tata Sons.
- Kishore Chaukar, Managing Director, Tata Industries.
- Arun Gandhi, Executive Director, Tata Sons.
- Alan Rosling, Executive Director, Tata Sons.

Commercial Importance

- **Tata Steel:** The sixth largest steel producer in the world and the largest steel producer in the private sector in India.
- **TCS:** Asia's largest software manufacturer.
- **Tata Tea:** The world's largest integrated tea company.

- **Tata Chemicals:** Largest in India and third largest soda ash producer in the world.
- **Tata Power:** India's largest energy company in the private sector.
- **Taj Group:** The largest chain of five-star luxury hotels in India.
- **Titan:** The world's fifth largest watch manufacturer.

First in India

- Establishment of the steel industry.
- Envisage and implement of labour-friendly rules, such as 8 hours of work, provident fund, gratuity, maternity benefit and all other facilities.
- Establishment of India's first power plant.
- Establishment of civil aviation.
- Start of insurance business.
- To establish a chain of luxury hotels in India.
- Production of commercial vehicles.
- Software development work.
- Production of Indica, the indigenous car of India.

Honors Received by Ratan Tata

- On 26 January 2008, he was awarded India's second highest civilian honor the 'Padma Vibhushan'.
- In 2008, he was awarded the 'NASSCOM Global Leadership Award-2008'.
- In 2007, Ratan Tata received the 'Carnegie Medal of Philanthropy' Award from the Tata family.
- In 2006, Cornell University honoured him with the 26th 'Robert S. Hetfield Fellow in Economics'.
- In 2004, Ratan Tata was awarded the title of 'Honorary Economic Advisor to Hangzhou City' in China.
- He has received the titles of honorary doctorate from London School of Economics and Indian Institute of Technology, Kharagpur.
- In May 2008, he was ranked in Time magazine's list of 100 influential people in the world.
- On 29 August 2008, the Government of Singapore granted him Honorary Citizenship. The award was conferred on him for his contribution to the development of Singapore.

Earned Membership

- Member, Prime Minister's Council, Trade and Industry.
- Member, Advisory Board, Mitsubishi Corporation.
- Member, American International Group, J.P. Morgan and Booz Allen Hamilton.
- Member, Board of Trustees, RAND Corporation.
- Member, University of Southern California, Cornell University.
- Member, South Africa International Investment Council.
- Member, Asia-Pacific Advisory Committee on New York Stock Exchange.
- President, Indian Institute of Science Court, Bangalore.
- Secretary, Managing Committee, Tata Institute of Fundamental Research, Mumbai.
- Member, Global Business Council of HIV; For AIDS awareness related work in India.

Along with this he is associated with many other national and international organizations.

Paramount in Generosity

The money that Jamsetji and his sons earned during the industrialization of the country was not spent on their comfort and luxury. He put most of that money in the trusts for the welfare of the people, so that it can be used only for their welfare.

Earning money for yourself and earning for others are both opposite poles. But here the mention is of that business family which has earned money for its country through all the struggles, troubles and dangers and has formed and efficiently operated many trusts to spend it in the service of the countrymen in various ways.

Social Welfare Works of Jamsetji

The group which Jamsetji Tata started with the establishment of a textile factory in central India in 1870, is now famous in the country and abroad. Jamsetji's thought and vision led to the foundation of the textile industry as well as the steel and energy industries in the country. He laid the foundation for technical education, started public welfare works and thus paved the way for India to reach the gateway of 21st century.

After Jamsetji's death, his elder son Sir Dorabji Tata took charge of the Tata group and with the support his younger brother Sir Ratan Tata and uncle R.D. Tata he gave form to Jamsetji's dream.

The spirit of trusteeship is a kind of by-product of the business of Jamsetji and his sons, through which they had to meet the needs of the country. His extensive ideological thinking gave him the idea of doing something beyond his business interests and the determination to give a concrete form to it. The desire to develop his country as an industrialized nation was deeply rooted in Jamsetji. Along with this, he was filled with the passion to train the youth of our country. Under this idea, from 1892 onwards, he started sending deserving youth to study abroad by giving scholarships for higher education. When the British opened up the Indian Civil Service (equivalent to today's Indian Administrative Service) to the Indians for recruitment, it was his heartfelt desire that more Indians should join it. So he started giving scholarships to the worthy people. A survey in 1924 made it clear that out of every 5 Indian ICS at that time, one was a Tata Scholar. Among the people who were benefited from the Tata Endowment Fund at that time, few are- J.C. Koyaji, a member of the Viceroy's Executive, B.N. Rao, Chief Justice Bombay High Court, Dr. Jeevaraj N. Mehta (later Chief Minister of Gujarat), Dr. Raja Ramanna, K.R. Narayanan (later became President of India), V.V. Narlikar, J.V. Narlikar, etc.

◻◻

Contribution of Sir Ratan Tata

Jamsetji was fortunate in the fact that his sons also had similar rites. His younger son Ratan Tata was very kind and generous hearted and was always ready to help any person or institution in trouble. The national sentiment had merged with his personal views. He was a man of extensive and balanced views.

Charity or philanthropy is possible only when there is passion inside the person and he is deeply attached to any thought and action. Then only he can be willing to give time to it as well as cooperate and help financially. During his lifetime, Sir Ratan Tata had identified many cases where according to him there was need of cooperation and help.

Gopalakrishna Gokhale founded the 'Servants of India Society' in Poona in June 1905. His aim was to prepare selfless, intelligent workers for India. Such workers, who can devote their lives to the service of the country.

At the request of Gopalkrishna Gokhale, Sir Ratan Tata gave assistance of ₹ 10,000 every year to Gopalakrishna Gokhale's organization for ten years.

This amount was to be spent by the institution for the welfare of the weaker sections of the society.

Similarly, he also helped the non-cooperation movement being run by Mahatma Gandhi in South Africa. This movement was being carried out on the apartheid policy of the then British Government and the issue of mistreatment of the people of the Indian community. Like other patriots, Sir Ratan also believed that it was a legitimate and cooperative movement. The repression movement by the British government was in full swing against it.

On the appeal of cooperation by Mahatma Gandhi, Sir Ratan sent a sum of ₹ 1.25 lakh in instalments for five years from 1909 to 1913 to Gandhiji so that he could continue his movement.

Expressing his gratitude to Sir Ratan, Gandhiji said that his cooperation has led to the realization that India has now woken up. His help will prove to be a great force for our movement.

In 1912, Sir Ratan Tata proposed to help the University of London to set up a bench that suggested the causes of poverty and ways to overcome them. A plan was submitted by the university. A Chair (Peeth) was established in 1913 after Sir Ratan Tata's approval. Sir Ratan agreed to pay 1,400 pounds annually for this project for three years. In 1916, it was extended for the next five years. Even after the death of Sir Ratan Tata, the trust formed in his name continued to grant this bench till 1931. In these nineteen years, many scholars of the university did research work on the status of workers in various occupations and got it published. Today the 'Sir Ratan Tata Foundation' is a permanent institution at the London School of Economics.

Between 1913 and 1917, Sir Ratan gave an economic grant of ₹ 75,000 to implement the archaeological mining project of Pataliputra. As a result of this excavation, many items of archaeological importance were revealed. Items received are displayed in Patna's museum. This was his immense urge to bring national pride to the fore.

Sir Ratan Tata was also an admirer of art and culture. He was also an enthusiastic traveller, who travelled to many places in the country and abroad. During his travels, he collected many items of art and cultural importance. In 1919, the collection was valued at ₹ 5 lakh. After his death, according to his will this entire collection was transferred to the Prince of Wales Museum in 1921, where it is still on display.

This is just a specimen of the fulfilment of the social concerns of Sir Ratan. During his lifetime he did many works of philanthropy. These include assistance to victims of disasters like flood, famine, fire, earthquake etc. and periodic assistance to hospitals, monuments, schools and many other social utility institutions etc.

His approach on how to use a trust fund was quite clear. In 1913, he put forward an outline of it. According to him, all the fields of education, teaching and industry were within its scope and all the things of general public work were included in it. The employment of persons who were suitable and capable in reaching the depth of cases for social, economic and political fulfilment was its another feature. Along with this, he would agree to support any plan and experiment only when it was carefully prepared and considered on all aspects.

❑❑

Sir Ratan Tata Trust

After the death of Sir Ratan Tata in 1918, the Sir Ratan Tata Trust was set up with ₹ 80 lakh. It is one of the oldest grantors in India. After his death, the public welfare works carried out by him were continued by the trust formed in his name.

In 1995, a strategy was prepared for the activities of Sir Ratan Tata Trust from 1995 to 2000 under the leadership of Ratan Tata. It had to do something beyond the traditional welfare works so that these welfare works could be planned for national development.

For this, it was decided to focus on the following areas to provide grants-
♦ Rural Living and Community Areas
♦ Education
♦ Health
♦ Arts and culture
♦ Public initiative.

Under this, around 65 new grants were approved for the year 2000-2001 and the trust sanctioned grants worth about 16 crores for various works. This is just one example. In later years, the number of schemes offered and its monetary size increased.

After the introduction of the new strategy by Ratan Tata, the Trust has been providing major support to programs to improve the standard of living of the rural poor and the rural community.

Under this, special attention is being paid to the following areas-

♦ Non-agricultural works, help to the women groups notably.

♦ Rural community.

♦ Relief to communities suffering from natural disasters.

♦ Research on major problems in rural area.

♦ Emphasis on development of human resources in rural areas.

♦ Emphasis on proper management of resources to increase agricultural production.

In the field of education, the trust is focused on two main categories — 1. Schooling, 2. Higher education. The objective of the grants has been to support community education in this area. The main emphasis is also on quality education. It is an attempt to achieve this by increasing the level of knowledge of teachers by training and by paying adequate attention to the education being imparted in the classrooms. To keep the children in schools, various programs are being provided outside the school also. Special attention is also being given to value-based education.

The Trust is supporting community-based health programs in the health sector. For this, attention is also being given to cooperation of public and individual joint ventures and to develop an activist organization of public health professionals.

Various types of grants are being given to the art sector by the Sir Ratan Tata Trust for the safety and security of things of archaeological importance.

The Trust is also supporting such programs in which people of both the male and female sections are being made capable according to the changing social changes.

The trust is also providing grants to institutions working in some selected areas. The condition of the grant is only that the work has the desired effect on the society or it is a work of important nature in some area.

Along with the institutions, the trust is also giving grants to individual people and small institutions. This work is being done by 'Sir Ratan Tata Small Grants Program'. In this, grants are given mainly to small institutions engaged in welfare works and people working for educational and health purposes.

❏❏

Sir Dorabji Tata Trust

Sir Dorabji Tata Trust was established in 1932 by Dorabji, the elder son of Jamsetji Tata. Shortly before his death Dorabji had bequeathed this trust to his entire estate, which at that time was 1 crore rupees. It included his significant stakes of Tata Sons.

Although Sir Dorabji spent most of his time in fulfilling his father's big dreams, still he took out time for public welfare works. One of the two trusts he founded three months before his death was the Lady Tata Memorial Trust. It was of relatively small stature and was primarily for research in the area of leukemia. The second Sir Dorabji Tata Trust was of a large scale. It was due to the generosity of this trust that some of the leading institutions of India were established, such as-

1. Tata Institute of Social Sciences (1936).
2. Tata Memorial Hospital (1941).
3. Tata Institute of Fundamental Research (1945).
4. National Centre for Performing Arts (1966).

After the death of J.R.D., honouring his wish the Dorabji Tata Trust helped the M.S. Swaminathan Research Foundation to establish J.R.D. Tata Centre for Ecotechnology.

Jamsetji Tata had a strong desire to establish a 'School of Medical Research into Tropical Medicine'. Dorabji wanted to establish it in 1912 to honour his wish; But for some reasons this could not be possible then. The wish of the two was fulfilled in 1999, when the 'Sir Dorabji Tata Centre for Research in Tropical Diseases' was established at the Indian Institute of Science, Bangalore. In 2004, the Trust contributed in the establishment of the School of Rural Development, Tuljapur and Tata Medical Centre, Calcutta. From its beginning till 2006, the Trust distributed approximately 380 crore and all this was given to support creative work.

Apart from this, Tata Trusts are contributing in many areas in different parts of the country. A series of Tata trusts will be sufficient to demonstrate their work and scope. These are:

- Sir Ratan Tata Trust.
- Sir Dorabji Tata Trust.
- Jamsetji Tata Trust.
- J.N. Tata endowment.
- J.R.D. Tata Trust.
- The J.R.D. And Thelma J. Tata Trust.

- Lady Meherbai D Tata Education Trust.
- Lady Tata Memorial Trust.
- R. D. Tata Trust.
- M.K. Tata Trust.
- Tata Social Welfare Trust.
- Tata Education Trust.

The Tata group companies are also engaged at their levels in developing their surroundings and making lives of people happier. Not only this, they are involved in public welfare works even in remote areas of the country outside their region.

❏❏

Relief Work During Disasters

Tata's tradition of relief work during natural disasters began with the earthquake in Quetta in 1934. The specialty of the relief work done by Tata is that whether it is relief work or rehabilitation, they do all the work themselves with their own resources and through their people.

One example will be sufficient. In 1993, there was a great earthquake in Latur in the morning and a supreme meeting was called same day in the evening for relief work, but before the meeting itself, several groups of Tata employees had departed with adequate furnishings and materials to provide relief to the people of earthquake-affected area. Where else can one find such passion? Other employees donated blood and sent it for the victims. On this front, the Tata Relief Committee set up for the eastern part of the country, helped the earthquake victims just like the relief committee of its western part. The Relief Committee of the Western Region took up various relief and rehabilitation schemes and completed them. To live in these, construction of residential, establishment of schools and establishment of health centers are the main. The Sir Dorabji Tata Trust took up the task of establishing water facilities and improving the condition of agriculture and animals. Through the Relief and Rehabilitation Division of his Tata Relief Committee, Ratan Tata helped the government of Gujarat by constructing 22 schools in the earthquake affected Rapar taluka of Kutch. These school buildings are built to the best of engineering standards and are seismic.

Even during the Kargil War, as per its practice, Tata chose the path of functional cooperation, rather than merely concluding his duty by paying a check. Tata consulted with the Ministry of Defence and set up a special Tata Defence Welfare Corps Fund in the Ministry of Defence. In this, companies and employees of the Tata group donated an amount of Rs 12 crore.

This amount was not only to help the martyred or injured in Kargil or their family members, but also to help the victims of other wars and conflicts before it. It was also for the soldiers of the security forces who were in Sri Lanka conflict, counter insurgency, peace keeping work and those who became crippled due to war; for widows of the martyrs and for giving grants for higher education of their children. The officers of Tata and the Security Army used to meet for necessary allocation in every 6 months.

Ratan Tata is the chairman of the multi-purpose trusts of the Tata Group. The idea of creative work for Tata philanthropy is a revolutionary idea for the traditional charitable organizations whose work was only to donate. Today, the 'Tata family' is one of the family among the few philanthropists in the country, which is involved in the development of the country, battling with problems at the individual, local and national levels. Along with helping in the development of the country, Ratan Tata is associated with all the welfare works.

□□

Nano: Manufacturing of People's Car

The world's cheapest car project began in 2003 under Ratan Tata, chairman of Tata Motors. Ratan Tata got this inspiration from the troubles of millions of two-wheeler drivers who cannot afford expensive cars. Therefore, take necessary travels with their family of 3-4 members on a two-wheeler. In this way, they complete their journey by risking not only their own life but also of their entire family. Ratan Tata had a dream to build and deliver a car within their budget to ease their troubles. Tata made the necessary changes to the manufacturing process to meet its design criteria to make a low-budget car possible, emphasizing on innovation and it asked the suppliers to give form to new design concepts. The car was designed keeping in mind the changes suggested by Ratan Tata. As compared to the Maruti-800, the Nano has 21 percent more space inside it. According to CRISIL Rating Agency, the entry of Nano into the market would expand India's car business by 65 percent. Tata Motor has kept the initial price of the Nano at ₹ 1, 00, 000, hence it has also been called Lakhtakia car. It is the lowest priced car in the world. It can also be purchased by families with an annual income of 1 lakh rupees. In this sense it is actually a People's Car.

Tata Motors showcased the Nano model at the 9th Auto Expo on January 10, 2008. Due to the relatively low price and other features, it was a centre of attraction.

The Tata Nano is a small four-seater city car. Its engine is installed in the rear. It has been greatly appreciated due to its low price and environmental relative characteristics. The main idea is that the Tata group will produce the Nano on a large scale, especially its electric model. Along with sales in India, it will be exported worldwide. The car will be produced in one standard and two luxury models. This project to manufacture the world's cheapest car started in 2003 on the initiative of the Chairman of Tata Motors, Ratan Tata. The success of Tata Motors in the production of a mini truck in 2005 also inspired for the development of Nano.

Tata's initial goal was to produce the world's least expensive car, with a starting price of ₹ 100,000 and 2,300 dollars in the US dollars. This price remained despite the fact that the material price had risen by 13 to 23 percent within five years of developing the car.

Tata Nano's electric model is also expected to be in great demand overseas. Director General for Energy and Transport, European Commission Matthias Ruete is of the view that the entire Europe, like other countries, is eagerly awaiting the commercial marketing of Tata Nano. But considering the adverse effect of carbon dioxide on the environment, it would be more appropriate to develop an electric model of Nano.

Launch of Nano Project

In fact, the Nano project started in 2003 when Tata Motors formed a team of four members and asked them to complete a new project. The project was the development of a new four-wheeler traffic vehicle. At that time it was only said that it would cost ₹ 1,00,000. At that time the lowest priced car cost around 2.5 lakh rupees. It was also clarified that the trust and safety of the customers and environmental requirements have to be taken care of in this.

The design team considered several designs and looked at alternative methods of vehicle manufacturing and tried to draw some conclusions from the then small cars.

The team considered a number of options and situations, such as the use of plastic instead of metal, the decrease of internal space or the use of a low power engine. The focus at that time was to keep the price low. Various techniques were tried. But a question remains incomplete on how much the customer will be satisfied. When it was decided that the autorickshaw approach would not work for the development of a suitable car, other ideas emerged, such as- Doorless, where there is an iron door, cloth ceiling, plastic doors, etc.

But Ratan Tata did not agreed on any of these suggestions. He had a clear idea that a whole car was needed at a low price, not a car-like structure.

Many ideas were tried. Headlight in different shape, to give the front part of the car a child-like appearance-big eyes in small face etc. But Ratan Tata asked for something different. Repeated changes in the design was painful for the team.

A feature of New Indica was added to the Nano. This led to a change in the front volume of the Nano and with it a noticeable change was seen in the look of the car.

This was a delightful turn in the development of the car, as well as a director. Keeping in mind that the car should look big too and the wheels on the corners should give the car an attractive look on the road, a full-fledged shape was developed. Discussions were made on even the shape and location of the lower corner of the glass. In all these matters, discussions with Ratan Tata continued.

By July 2007, a model was almost settled and an idea to work on it was formulated at the initial stage. That's when Tata found the front of the car somewhat awkward, so Tata decided to increase it. A new design was made and presented to Ratan Tata in late August, same year, which he immediately approved.

Now it was the turn of the interior design of the car. There was ample scope for changes here compared to traditional designs. Here too the question was of low cost, but there was no dispute in making it comfortable. The main task was to balance the cost of the car to suit customer satisfaction as well as the market. Along with this, the space inside the car had to be used in such a way that it would look attractive. Many ideas came up for this. They were implemented after enough deliberation on the proper suggestions and an attractive shape could be given to the interior of the car.

As this task was completely different from the traditional auto engineering, a variety of problems cropped up at each step of manufacturing, such as installing the engine in the rear instead of the front. This was a unique idea. This increased space inside the car, but hindered the balance problem. Some setups had to be brought forward accordingly. They were reconciled with the respective setups and then the trial tested its quality and efficiency. Reforms and trials took place if any deficiency was found. The floor channel was changed ten times to meet the prescribed parameters. Similarly, the dashboard and seats were also changed almost the same number of times. But the team was busy in their work, because the feeling of doing something new and unique and the inspiration and direction of Ratan Tata was with them.

In fact, the idea of installing the engine of the car in the rear proved revolutionary for the design process. A team to raise resources for a 35 horse power engine suitable for city cars travelled all the countries of the world but, no such engine was found, which was within the budget of the car. Then an engine manufactured by Tata Motors itself was tested, which was not found suitable for the Nano. In the end the Fiat Bosch Electronics Company's engine eventually passed the trial for the Nano and was approved.

Installing the engine, gear box and exhaust system behind the rear seats was a difficult task. This was efficiently accomplished by the engineering team. The engineering team should also be appreciated for the fact that it designed and installed many new structures for the Nano.

A production team formed over the next few months after the design process was completed. This work was done neatly. Apart from Tata Motors, people were also taken from outside. Among them were graduate trainee engineers of IIT, Kharagpur and Jadavpur University. Overall, it was a mixed team, a combination of experience and youthful enthusiasm. This combined fresh ideas with experience and heralded a new work culture.

The car manufacturing process is a rigorous process. It is not easy to do it on your own with a few people or companies. Therefore, the role of other companies and vendors is important in this, which prepares and supplies all kinds of products required in car manufacturing. It is easy to get the work done or done according to the traditional process and specifications, but creating a new pool of vendors for a new concept car like the Nano or persuading the elders to make the products according to the needs of the car was a difficult task, which was resolved by communicating with them and by providing necessary technology, design and guidance. Therefore, a group of about 100 vendors was formed to support Nano production which could design and supply products according to the need and can form part of the Nano production process and make the production of cars on a large scale possible.

Singur Land Acquisition Dispute

Tata Motors chose West Bengal to set up the Nano project. This could pave the way for the establishment of industries in West Bengal along with providing employment to a large number of people. People's income would have increased, because many other industries were likely to be established there, excited by the success of the Nano project. It could eradicate poverty for many rural people by providing employment.

Land for the establishment of factory was acquired in the Singur region of Bengal. This process of land acquisition went well and the land owners were also satisfied about the amount of compensation. But during this process, a section of landowners, who did not live there, some illiterate farmers and activists of Trinamool Congress, a political party, raised a dispute by refusing to accept this compensation amount. Due to the spread of politics, many new dimensions started giving vent to this dispute. Some started calling it a fertile agricultural land, while few others started hue and cry on the compensation of lesser amount. While some questioned the legitimacy of the acquisition of land, some made it a matter of forcibly acquiring it.

Although, the West Bengal government wholeheartedly wanted the Nano project to take place in his state. It created the necessary environment for this and facilitated the acquisition of about 997 acres of land.

Mamta Banerjee's Trinamool Congress and Socialist Unity Centre were at the forefront in opposing the land acquisition. He was given full support by civil and human rights groups, legal institutions and social workers, who are always keen to help on such opportunities.

Those opposing it had to face criticism and verbal warnings from the state ruling party C.P.I. (M) and scuffles by its activist. Survey officials of the state government and Tata Motors faced heavy resistance at the hands of members of the 'Singur Krishi Bhoomi Bachao Samiti'.

As a result, the state government had to issue prohibitory orders under section 144 of the Indian Penal Code; but the Calcutta High Court declared it illegal.

The government took control of the land earmarked for the project and began its siege in Tarabad in December 2006 amid protests. In protest to this, Mamta Banerjee called for a state-wide shutdown and later started a 25-day hunger strike. Members of her party vandalized the assembly. A large number of police forces and activists of the Marxist Party started guarding the area inside Tarabad, but the siege continued to be attacked intermittently by the opposing villagers and other groups. In January 2007, the factory construction work started on the allotted land. But the resistance against it was not being stopped, but rather it grew furious day by day. Due to this, the work of giving practical shape to the project program was stopped and precious time was lost.

Seeing the establishment of the Nano project fail in West Bengal, other states started efforts to pull it into their state. In the meantime, efforts were made to compromise and to find a middle path. But no effective solution came out so that the entire project could be implemented in one place. Rather than succumb to the pressures, Ratan Tata decided to withdraw from Singur and announced it on 2 October 2008.

◻◻

New Centre for Setting Up Nano Project: Sanand (Gujarat)

After spending a lot of time and resources in West Bengal, Tata announced shifting its Lakhtakia car Nano project to Sanand near Ahmedabad in Gujarat. 2,000 crores were to be spent on this project. But along with it, decision was made to produce it from another centre for delivery of the car on time. It is another matter that prior to this announcement, there was a round of silent talks between the Government of Gujarat and the Tata representatives. A letter of consent was finally signed between the State Secretary of Industry and the Managing Director of Tata Motors. In this agreement, the Chief Minister of the state, Narendra Modi, also played an effective role, who ensured the rapid allocation of 1,100 acres of good standing land. Ratan Tata himself thanked for this. Nearly 60 vendors, along with Tata Motors, also turned to Sanand to play a supporting role in Nano production.

It has now been decided that Tata Nano will be mass-produced from a factory set up in Sanand, Gujarat.

Meanwhile, the production of Nano started at a relatively low level at the Pantnagar plant, where some production lines of a truck were converted to conform to Nano production. Similarly, Tata Motors' Pune plant also started to work on some production lines to ensure the entry of Nano into the market at the scheduled time.

The annual production capacity of the Sanand plant will be 2,50,000 units, which will be extended later.

☐☐

Entry of Nano in the Market

Overcoming all the challenges, Tata Motors of Ratan Tata finally made the Nano run on the Indian roads in July 2009, when its first customer was handed the car key. Ashok Raghunath, one of the first three customers of Nano, was handed the car key by Chairman Ratan Tata himself. It was silver colour of the Nano LX model. The commencement of the process of handing over the car to customers on time despite the precious time wasted due to the Singur controversy was a good sign for both Nano and Tata Motors.

Nano: Some facts

Technical and other features

- Rear wheel drive.
- Two-cylinder 623 cc rear engine 33 PS. Car (single balancer shaft).
- Fuel Consumption 4.55 L / 100 km (21.97 km / L, city condition, normal 20 km / L).
- Length 3.1 m.
- Height 1.6 m.
- Width 1.5 m.

Safety: All sheet metal body, intrusion resistant doors, seat belts, tubeless tires. The car has successfully passed full frontal crash and side impact crash standards.

Environmentally friendly: Reduced pollution levels from two-wheelers being built in India. Reduction in carbon dioxide emissions due to high fuel efficiency.

Nano has successfully passed all the standards set by the government to take vehicles on the road.

The Nano will have three models—the first standard model, two higher-end models that will fit the air conditioner. The RCX will be of 600 kg of these three early models and the LX will be of 615 and 635 kg respectively.

Nano-Europe is expected to be introduced in the market by 2011.

Ratan Tata: A Gentle and Dignified Personality

Ratan Tata is also known for his gentleness and humility. He is counted among the leading businessmen of the world, but still with no sense of pride. He is unmarried and the entire Tata family is like a family to him. It would have been difficult for him to make time for his personal family in the preparation of this family; but instead of establishing a separate family, he has raised the entire Tata Empire as a family. He drives his own car to go to his office. He travels alone even on trips of long commercial nature. He does not like caboodle. In India he like to fly his own plane. He is a skilled pilot. At the 'Aero India Exhibition' in 2007, he surprised everyone by flying as a co-pilot in the fighter aircraft F-16 and Boeing F-18.

His dealings with his subordinates are tempered with tenderness. Subordinates also look at him with an eye of affection and respect. In personal life, he is a fearless man with strong intentions. It is not possible to bow him down because he is firm in his thoughts. He is alert to the dangers, but does not change his path fearing them. It is his nature to accept challenges. He has established the Tata Group as a commercial superpower on the global scene. After 2003, he has made a series of acquisitions and commercial agreements.

He bought his truck manufacturing unit from South Korea's Daewoo Motors. Whether it is the case of Indonesia's largest coal mine or the steel mills of Singapore, Thailand and Vietnam, he is making his mark everywhere. In addition, he gained control of Pierre in New York, Ritz-Carlton in Boston and Campton Place in San Francisco through his Indian Hotels Group.

In 2004, he bought Tyco International's global undersea telecom cables for $ 130 million. Thus, the Tata group rose to the top of the world as an 'international call carrier'. With the purchase of British engineering firm Incat International, Tata Technologies has become a major supplier in the field of 'outsourced industrial design' to American auto and auto space companies. The subsequent acquisition of Dutch-British steel company Corus is a major achievement in itself. In one stroke, Tata Steel increased its finished product and reached out to auto makers in the US and Europe. With this registered a five-fold increase in its capacity. The market value of listed Tata companies has gone from $ 12 billion to $ 62 billion. Similarly, the sales and profit levels of the group have also gone up and it has crossed the figure of $29 billion and $2.8 billion respectively.

Tata Steel, Tata Motors and Tata Consultancy Services generate 75 percent of revenue from total sales.

With the purchase of the Jaguar Land Rover brand, Tata has made a significant presence in the luxury car market.

He has introduced a new dimension of his skill and vision by building the world's lowest priced car. He is also looking forward at American aeronautics in the future. He has tied up with the American company Sikorsky to set up a helicopter manufacturing factory in Hyderabad.

Ratan Tata wants Tata companies to prove that they can compete with companies in developed countries and stay steadfast in emerging markets.

Along with this, they are also discharging social responsibilities with utmost preparedness. Tata group is also devoted to public welfare work. He is doing this through his various trusts. These charitable trusts hold about 66 percent of Tata Sons' shares. Tata entered into the retail, telecom, biotech and other sectors by gaping from the marginal business companies, which were involved in the cosmetics, paints and cement business and made a strong footprint in many areas.

Today the Tata Group has around 100 companies and 300 ancillaries, which are trading in 40 businesses. The group is threaded together through limited employees of the holding company—Tata Sons and Tata Industries. Both these holding companies are working under the chairmanship of Ratan Tata. These two companies only work as controller of strategic vision and Tata based. These companies help in big agreements. Bombay House, a group corporate office set up by Ratan Tata, also leaves its mark on these companies. The nine senior executives of Tata companies are members of the board of the Tata company, which discharges corporate responsibility. Ratan Tata participates in major agreements as chief executive.

Ratan Tata's role in the Corus Agreement was pioneering. This was a large level of work and the amount of money involved was also very large. Yet Ratan Tata preserved unwavered. He had faith in himself and his group.

The Tata Steel Company spends millions of rupees annually on about 800 villages around the site of the establishment, which are spent on projects such as education, health and agricultural development.

Jamshedpur, established in 1908, is home to about 7,00,000 people today, with a Tata workforce of around 20,000. Despite this, Tata Steel has carried the responsibility of all public facilities and schools in the city.

Ratan Tata is a person of calm nature. Always away from publicity, he does his work silently without attracting the attention of the people. He buys companies and brands around the world. In this way, he has transformed a family group into a multinational company today. In July 2009, when US Secretary of State Hillary Clinton came to India, she expressed her condolences to the victims of the 26/11 terrorist attacks in a booklet of condolences kept there. In the Taj Hotel itself, she discussed matters of mutual interest with selected Indian industrialists and some important personalities of the business world. Ratan Tata himself was the host of this meeting.

❏❏

Something More about Ratan Tata

Who can forget the 26/11 terror attack in Mumbai, when ten terrorists crossed the Indian maritime border into Mumbai and fired indiscriminately at many places and killed many people? But many people may not know what the Tata group did for its employees affected by the attack.

The Tata group considered all categories of employees, including those working as temporary employees for day, on duty while the hotel was closed.

Employees' salaries were sent by money order during the hotel closure. Not only this, a psychiatric unit was also established to provide counselling facilities to the needy in collaboration with the Tata Institute of Social Sciences. A mentor was assigned to each employee and it was the responsibility of the person to act as a 'single window clearance' for all the help the employee sought. Ratan Tata himself met the families of 80 employees injured or dead in this attack. Ratan Tata himself asked these family members and dependents what kind of help they expect from him.

In a record time of twenty days, the Tata group formed a trust aimed at helping employees. The unique thing in this was that other people affected by the attack, such as railway employees, police personnel, people walking on the pavement, who had no connection with the Tatas', were also brought under compensation. During this attack, many vendors who lost their means of livelihood were provided with hand carts by Tata.

All senior managers, including Ratan Tata, were busy in the last visit (antim yatra) of the dead for three consecutive days. It was a really terrible phase. The provided facilities mentioned below, in terms of each of its deceased employees by Tata costed in range from ₹ 36 to 85 lakh.

1. The lifetime amount equal to the last salary of the employee to family and dependents.
2. To take full responsibility for the education of dependents and children anywhere in the world.
3. Lifetime medical care to the whole family and dependents.
4. All debts and advance payments are forgiven— no matter how large the amount.
5. Lifelong counselling facility for every person.

Mantra is that if you care about your employees then the employees will also give their life for your product. Companies thinking of employee interest never have to face a problem like holding them back.

(Sincerely: N. Raghuraman, 'Dainik Bhaskar')

Reference

1. www.tata.com
2. www.srtt.org
3. www.tatamotors.com
4. www.businessworld.in
5. www.deshgujarat.com
6. www.daylife.com
7. www.team-bhp.com
8. www.livemint.com
9. www.photogallery.outlookindia.com
10. www.pmindia.nic.in
11. www.thesagefoundation.com

Top Motivational Quotes/Inspiring

1. Always deliver more than expected.
2. Apart from values and ethics which I have tried to live by, the legacy I would like to leave behind is a very simple one - that I have always stood up for what I consider to be the right thing, and I have tried to be as fair and equitable as I could be.
3. At Tatas, we believe that if we are not among the top three in an industry, we should look seriously at what it would take to become one of the top three players or think about exiting the industry.
4. Banana republics are run on cronyism.
5. Britain needs a real push. It needs nationalism. The sort of spirit that comes during a war.
6. Business needs to go beyond the interest of their companies to the communities they serve.
7. Challenges need to be given to an organization.
8. Chase the vision, not the money, the money will end up following you.
9. Companies that do not will undoubtedly die.

10. Don't play games that you don't understand, even if you see lots of other people making money from them.
11. Don't take too much advice. Most people who have a lot of advice to give — with a few exceptions — generalize whatever they did. Don't over-analyze everything.
12. Every time we launch a feature, people yell at us.
13. Everyone thinks only about his profit.
14. Get big quietly, so you don't tip off potential competitors.
15. Governance is an important thing, not an application where it suits one so, to micro-control where it suits them on the other hand.
16. Having said that, I hope that a hundred years from now we will spread our wings far beyond India.
17. I admire very successful people. But if that success has been achieved through too much ruthlessness, then I may admire that person, but I can't respect him.
18. I am proud of my country. But we need to unite to make a unified India, free of communalism and casteism.
19. I came seriously close to getting married four times, and each time I backed off in fear or for one reason or another. Each occasion was different, but in hindsight when I look at the people involved, it wasn't a bad thing what I did. I think it may have been more complex had the marriage taken place.

20. I do not know how history will judge me, but let me say that I've spent a lot of time and energy trying to transform the Tatas from a patriarchal concern to an institutional enterprise.
21. I don't believe in taking right decisions.
22. I followed someone who had very large shoes. He had very large shoes. Mr. J.R.D. Tata. He was a legend in the Indian business community. He had been at the helm of the Tata organization for 50 years. You were almost starting to think he was going to be there forever.
23. I have always been very confident and very upbeat about the future potential of India. I think it is a great country with great potential.
24. I have been constantly telling people to encourage people, to question the unquestioned and not to be ashamed to bring up new ideas, new processes to get things done.
25. I have two or three cars that I like, but today, Ferrari would be the best car I have driven in terms of being an impressive car.
26. I may have hurt some people along the way, but I would like to be seen as somebody who has done his best to do the right thing for any situation and not compromised.
27. I take decisions and then make them right.
28. I think the environment has become more competitive. That has made the Indian industry more concerned with a) its customers, b) the quality of its products, and c) its brand image in the marketplace.

29. I think the Tata Group's greatest contribution to the growth of the Indian economy and Indian industry probably happened in the pre-independence era.
30. I think there are many honest businessmen.
31. I think you can have certain specific rules for engaging with India... for example, not allowing mineral resources to be taken out of the country... but there is not a shred of doubt in my mind that when you open an economy you should do it in totality.
32. I will certainly not join politics.
33. I would like to be remembered as a clean businessman who has not partaken in any twists and turns beneath the surface, and one who has been reasonably successful.
34. I would say that one of the things I wish I could do differently would be to be more outgoing.
35. I, for one, am not the kind who loves dwelling on the 'I'.
36. Ideas are easy. Implementation is hard.
37. If history remembers me at all, I hope it will be for this transformation.
38. If it stands the test of public scrutiny, do it... if it doesn't stand the test of public scrutiny then don't do it.
39. If people like you, they'll listen to you, but if they trust you, they'll do business with you.

40. If there are challenges thrown across, then some interesting, innovative solutions are found. Without challenges, the tendency is to go on the same way.

41. If you are not embarrassed by the first version of your product, you've launched too late.

42. If you want to walk fast, walk alone. But if you want to walk far, walk together

43. If you're interested in the living heart of what you do, focus on building things rather than talking about them.

44. If your actions inspire others to dream more, learn more, do more and become more, you are a leader.

45. India has probably lost its position to China as the world's workshop. At the same time, it has the power to be ahead of China when it comes to knowledge. Not that the Chinese are far behind. They will get there.

46. Indian car buyers have not been exposed to customer care in a competitive environment.

47. IT and the entire communications business have the greatest growth potential. But if you're talking about sheer size, the steel and auto industries will remain at the top.

48. It needs people really to want to see the UK sitting again, maybe not as a colonial power, but as an economic power.

49. It would, therefore, be a mark of failure on my part if it were perceived that Ratan Tata epitomises the Group's success.

50. It's not about ideas. It's about making ideas happen.

51. I've never believed protectionism of that kind will lead us anywhere.

52. Jardine is the largest dealer of Mercedes in the world. They also sell cars for two or three Japanese makers.

53. Make every detail perfect and limit the number of details to perfect.

54. Modesty is necessary, even if there is also a need for a certain amount of national pride. When it comes down to it, we have managed our country's economy poorly for long enough.

55. My concern is that the government doesn't appear to care about manufacturing.

56. None can destroy iron, but its rust can! Likewise, none can destroy a person, but its mindset can!

57. Nothing works better than just improving your product.

58. One hundred years from now, I expect the Tatas to be much bigger than it is now. More importantly, I hope the Group comes to be regarded as being the best in India... best in the manner in which we operate, best in the products we deliver and best in our value systems and ethics.

59. One of the weaknesses of the Indian industry is that zin many areas... like consumer goods... it is very fragmented. Individually, companies might not be able to survive.

60. Our challenge is to invest sufficiently in education.

61. People of great power wield great power, but people of lesser power or people who have fallen out of power go to jail without adequate evidence, or their bodies are found in the trunks of cars.

62. People still believe what they read is necessarily the truth.

63. Power and wealth are not two of my main stakes.

64. Some foreign investors accuse us of being unfair to shareholders by using our resources for community development. Yes, this is money that could have made for dividend payouts, but it also is money that's uplifting and improving the quality of life of people in the rural areas where we operate and work. We owe them that.

65. Some people dream of success, while other people get up every morning and make it happen.

66. Take the stones people to throw at you, and use them to build a monument.

67. The country is now universally recognised as a nation on the move and takes its place amongst the successful economies in the region.

68. The day I am not able to fly will be a sad day for me.

69. The early Rockefellers made their wealth from being in certain businesses and remained personally very wealthy. Tata's were different in the sense the future generations were not so wealthy. They were involved in the business but most of the family wealth was put into the trust

and most of the family did not enjoy enormous wealth.

70. The fastest way to change yourself is to hang out with people who are already the way you want to be.

71. The foreign investment adds a sense of competition; we should see this as a wake-up call to modernise and upgrade.

72. The future potential is enormous but the country's destiny is in our hands.

73. The government should do its job. The government's job is to run the country, to manage the country, to govern the country.

74. The Group's investments in industries such as steel, textiles, power and hotels were certainly driven by an entrepreneurial spirit, but they were driven, even more, I think, by a desire to make India self-sufficient and independent of its colonial masters then.

75. The political system of the People's Republic of China can make things easy. Decisions are made quickly and results come quickly, too. In our democracy (in India), on the other hand, such things are extremely difficult.

76. The strong life and the weak die. There is some bloodshed, and out of it emerges a much leaner industry, which tends to survive.

77. The Telco is committed to commercial vehicles, where it is bound to remain a major player. What

may well happen in the future is we may split the company into two business units.

78. The time has come for performance to be measured and for allocated funds of the government to reach the people for whom they were intended.

79. The time has come to move from small increments to bold, large initiatives.

80. The time has come to stretch the envelope and set goals which were earlier not seen to be possible.

81. The value of an idea lies in the using of it.

82. There are many things that, if I have to relive, maybe I will do it another way. But I would not like to look back and think about what I have not been able to.

83. There is no reason to now think that we can conquer the world.

84. Ups and downs in life are very important to keep us going because a straight line even in an ECG means we are not alive.

85. We can be a truly great nation if we set our sights high and deliver to the people the fruits of continued growth, prosperity and equal opportunity.

86. We have provinces, we have the rule of law, and we have a system of justice. But those are also weaknesses when compared with China. On the other hand, one of our strengths is that we are very individualistic, and as individuals, we are very creative. But that, too, is a weakness, because it keeps us from working well together.

87. We like to say that India has the advantage of being a large market.
88. We live in a highly competitive world and we Indians have to struggle to catch up.
89. We need to build India into a land of equal opportunity for all.
90. We need to stop taking baby steps and start thinking globally. It seems to be helping.
91. We're responsible for the fortunes of the company but this is a bone-dry situation in terms of access to credit. Nobody can operate on that basis unless you have large cash balances, which we don't.
92. What are the crumple zones on scooters? The helmet is the only crumple zone I can think of.
93. What do you need to start a business? Three simple things: know your product better than anyone, know your customer, and have a burning desire to succeed.
94. What I have done is to establish growth mechanisms, play down individuals and play up the team that has made the companies what they are.
95. What I would like to do is to leave behind a sustainable entity of a set of companies that operate in an exemplary manner in terms of ethics, values and continue what our ancestors left behind.
96. What is needed is a consortium of like companies in one industry, presenting a strong front to the

multinationals. The Swiss watch industry did this.

97. When you find an idea that you just can't stop thinking about, that's probably a good one to pursue.

98. When you see in places like Africa and parts of Asia abject poverty, hungry children and malnutrition around you, and you look at yourself as being people who have well being and comforts, I think it takes a very insensitive, tough person not to feel they need to do something.

99. Wonder what your customer wants? Ask. Don't tell.

100. Young entrepreneurs will make a difference in the Indian ecosystem.

Success Principles of Ratan Tata

We all have heard a lot about the Tata Group. Ratan Tata does not need any introduction due to his popularity in industrial circles, for the group's achievements and being the most successful pioneers of India. He is famous in the start-up circles for inspiring the youth through his life, philosophy and especially the dynamism with which he overturned the failure of many companies to churn a profit, making the conglomerate hugely successful. The Group has had great wealth and potential which has allowed it to grow by leaps and bounds in its lifetime. Tata once said that ups and downs are essential in one's life because even a straight line in the ECG machine conveys lifelessness. He reminds youth that, it is all the way more important to rise in the long term while facing any short terms ups and downs. In today's time, it is hard to find an industrialist who could show the youth a light like this which instils the very idea that life is always uncertain for everyone. As most of the individuals in the era of social media do believe that all problems of the world are just an ongoing hashtag, and all the rest are doing their best in their respective lives. This unrealistic gap between virtual and real life is one of the reasons for the rising depression rates in India.

He was born on December 28, 1937, in Surat, to Naval and Sonoo Tata. Naval Tata was the adopted son of Jamsetji Ji and Ratan Tata was raised by his paternal grandmother after his parents' separation. Although they remained in contact, Ratan could never get the love, indulgence, support or the upbringing from his own parents. He was very much close to his grandmother, who looked after him and raised him. She was a strict woman with a disciplined approach to life and tasks. He does signify the ideal of disciplined approach in business due to which JRD Tata had overlooked many seniors and appointed Ratan Tata as the chairman of the Tata Group in 1991.

After having completed his studies in India, he went to the US and applied at Cornell University, graduating in the field of Architecture, securing a B.S. degree in Architecture and Structural Engineering in 1962. He obtained an offer from IBM, worked over for 15 days and returned to India when he got to know about the adverse health of his grandmother, who was the most important person in his life. During his stay in the US, he was a living a life of any ordinary international student. He worked at different levels of 'so-called' small and big tasks to earn his money. He never wanted to return to India and still admires the US and the right time that he spent in the country. During his stay in India, JRD Tata got him convinced to work for his family business. He applied at the Harvard Business School and pursued an Advanced Management Program in 1975.

The mission and motto of the Tata Group have always been to develop India through industrialisation.

When the English East India Company's rule ended, and the British Raj was established after the First War of Independence in 1857, the terms and conditions for Indian exporters were relatively more liberal than during the reign of the company rule. Tata went around the world to see the best industrial practices and returned to India and invested in the same models and programs. Jamsetji Tata began his business venture from a textile unit and in over 150 years; the Group has grown into more than 30 companies across ten business verticals, including over 100 enterprises operating in over 100 countries under the group name. This signifies that businesses are run based on the ethos, attitude, and a rightful approach.

Tata Sons have great potential because of which we see a rise of industrial glories. Yet, Tata is not counted as one of the world's richest person. The Group uses 66% of its profit in philanthropy, and their business models are based on providing quality services to consumers. One of the best perks in the industrial sector is given over to their employees. This was merit on which the Tata Group was founded, and Tata has taken it forward in a huge way.

Mr. Tata once said, "Take the stones people throw at you and use them to build a monument". He proved his words right himself. In 1999, after the failure of Tata Indica due to various technical faults Mr. Tata decided to sell off the passenger vehicle company in 1999. While he was at Detroit to finalise the deal, then Head of Ford, Bill Ford and his team made humiliating remarks against Ratan Tata's idea and dream to develop cars suitable for India. He flew home and decided to heavily invest in Tata Motors to make it rise and shine. After clearing out the technical faults in Tata Indica which was his first indigenously developed Tata car for Indians. The company launched the second generation of the vehicle called as Tata Indica V2. It was a success this time. It was a viral experiment to develop a diesel engine for a five-seater car. Later, almost after nine years, the same Tata Motors took over JLR, i.e. Jaguar Land Rover Company from Bill Ford. One may wonder had Mr. Tata given up to Bill Ford then the course of history would never have been this exciting.

He was appointed the director in-charge of NELCO which stands for 'National Radio and Electronics Company Limited'. The main job of Mr. Tata was to help its struggling finances. He actively worked towards attaining financial and production line efficiency. The attempts were halted by Labour Union strikes and the economic recession to overhaul the unit. It was a big enterprise with just a 2% market share when Mr. Tata joined. After having dedicated ten years of hard work, debts were settled, and it turned into a profit-making unit. He had understood and realised that any advancement in a company could only be made with the introduction of the latest Science and Technology. Soon NELCO acquired 20% market share in the radio sector. Later the company manufactured inverters for housing units. During his stint at NELCO, JRD Tata was closely watching him. Being impressed with Mr. Tata's performance, the Board of Tata Group was confident about his takeovers of all loss-making units, which did start churning profit in a short period. It was in 1991 that JRD Tata got him appointed as the new chairman of the Tata Group of Companies. After his takeover, he turned most of the loss-making enterprises into profit-making ones. He was thereby succeeding in expanding the scope of financial viability and feasibility of running multiple companies under the group. He mainly transformed the managements, and brought in a vision of division of labour for efficiency, and helped him do what he had wanted.

In the 1980s, the then PM, Rajiv Gandhi's mindset was also technical and believed in the necessity of scientific temperament in terms of taking the country forward through industrialisation premised on technological developments. When he heard about Mr. Tata's strategies, he assured of his support to him. He made attempts to collaborate with Bill Gates and IBM, and the nation saw the computer and engineering sector getting a boost.

He got Tata Tea to acquire the teabag making company called as Tetley. Tata Steel acquired Corus. He tried to consolidate the same in the year 2000. In 2001, he launched the insurance company called Tata AIG, in partnership with an American Insurance Company. In 2003, TCS, i.e. Tata Consultancy Services, became the first Indian software company cross the threshold of earning more than 1 billion US Dollars in its revenue kitty. He received the Padma Bhushan in 2000 and Padma Vibhushan in 2008, the third and the second highest civilian awards conferred by the Government of India respectively. It was in 2008 that JLR was acquired in an all-cash deal. He also favoured consolidation of companies by using one Tata logo at all of its business units in operation. In 2006, he conceptualized the small car concept to favour a qualitative change into the lives of Indians. Tata Nano did not do well. However, he did everything to bring that concept into life successfully. He is called as a philanthropist because the Tata Trust spends 66% of his profits for CSR initiatives again for the same mission to develop the country and bring a quality change into lives of the ordinary people. They have always donated generously during every natural disaster or a calamity. The Group announced an INR 1500 Crore fund for COVID-19 relief. These examples highlight the success of the Tata Group under the chairmanship of Mr. Tata and the sheer dynamism and persona held by Mr. Tata.

He was well aware that his success lies in the ethos that he and his predecessors followed in life. Thus, he announced infusion of 5 principles as a Code of Conduct under all companies in The Group, i.e. Integrity, Understanding, Unity, Responsibility and Excellence based on the premise of equality. He believed that if he could get the employees to follow a specific protocol/code, then not only the group would excel due to the baseline underscoring the ideal of team spirit and values-based work culture. He felt this would bring a better and lasting change in the local level leadership of his company and employees. Many factors have made Mr. Tata what he is today; some of his Success Mantras are:

1. **Adjusting with life:** Mr. Tata though born and raised in a good family, saw what no child should see, i.e. separation of his parents. Yet he adjusted and adapted well growing up with his grandparents. While he was in the US, he didn't live a lavish life. On his return to India, he understood the value of the opportunity to take part in the family business, when JRD Tata persuaded him not to return abroad, giving up

his ambitions in a way to continue his dream job at IBM. Later, after having made NELCO a profit-making unit, all the loss-making units were transferred to him. The world saw the best of Mr. Tata when all the loss-making companies transferred to him started performing well. He has proved that in the course of life, there are many ups and downs. The need, however, is to quickly adapt to those changes and make the best out of oneself and the situation, to bring success and passion in the pursuit of life.

2. **Ethos:** Mr. Tata was raised by his grandmother, and she instilled a sense of discipline in him. JRD Tata saw this efficacy in practice yielding good results. Thus, he was made the chairman in 1991. If he were a man of casual attitude and flexible values, then Tata Group would have been very different today. For instance, when Bill Ford tried to insult Mr. Tata, he was determined to take sweet revenge by proving to the world that Tata Motors needed no mercy. This negative episode of his life further strengthened him never to sell out any Tata unit; for this, he ensured the best practices were followed among the employees and the employers.

3. **Good Will and Perseverance:** Mr. Tata always took pride in the legacy of his group. He never displayed any ego or showed off what he has got. He is a lone guy with no family and lives with two dogs, offers shelter to stray dogs in bad weather. This is the goodwill that he carries with himself. In every testing or challenging time in his life, he has never given up, and the result is, under his tenure of chairmanship revenues grew 40 fold

and profit by 50 times. If one can learn from him to never give up and keep following the integral path of goodwill in personal and professional life, then its results can be phenomenal.

4. **Caring for employees:** The Tata Group and Mr. Tata especially, always understood that employees could make or break the company. They offer their hard work, time and energy because of which the Group operates. Thus, one reason for his success is the fact that when it comes to offering perks and welfare to employees, they follow the most excellent practices. It is to the extent to keep high satisfaction and happiness levels in them to ensure the best productivity ratios. It fulfils the integral aspect of running the Tata Group, i.e. broader humanitarian welfare through a qualitative change in people's life.

5. **Learning from the West:** Mr. Tata ensured to follow the principle that worked the best for Tata Group, i.e. Learning from the West. Mr. Tata was aware in the post-liberalization era and rising privatization, the competition would come through the channels of Globalisation. He ensured the best science and technology was used to create synergies and produce quality products. He heavily invested on the subject of innovation and. It is this subject that has driven the change under the era of Mr. Tata making him all the way more successful, so much that today every Indian takes pride to enjoy the luxury and comfort of a 5 star rated Global NCAP cars, which is above and beyond all the safety parameters of safety stipulated by the Government of India.

❏❏